Learn Spanish with La Puerta De Bronce and Other Stories

HypLern Interlinear Project
www.hyplern.com

First edition: 2025, October

Author: Manuel Romero De Terreros
Translation: Kees van den End
Foreword: Camilo Andrés Bonilla Carvajal PhD

ISBN: 978-1-988830-85-8

kees@hyplern.com
www.hyplern.com

Learn Spanish with La Puerta De Bronce and Other Stories

Interlinear Spanish to English

Author
Manuel Romero De Terreros

Translation
Kees van den End

HypLern Interlinear Project
www.hyplern.com

The HypLern Method

Learning a foreign language should not mean leafing through page after page in a bilingual dictionary until one's fingertips begin to hurt. Quite the contrary, through everyday language use, friendly reading, and direct exposure to the language we can get well on our way towards mastery of the vocabulary and grammar needed to read native texts. In this manner, learners can be successful in the foreign language without too much study of grammar paradigms or rules. Indeed, Seneca expresses in his sixth epistle that "Longum iter est per praecepta, breve et efficax per exempla[1]."

The HypLern series constitutes an effort to provide a highly effective tool for experiential foreign language learning. Those who are genuinely interested in utilizing original literary works to learn a foreign language do not have to use conventional graded texts or adapted versions for novice readers. The former only distort the actual essence of literary works, while the latter are highly reduced in vocabulary and relevant content. This collection aims to bring the lively experience of reading stories as directly told by their very authors to foreign language learners.

Most excited adult language learners will at some point seek their teachers' guidance on the process of learning to read in the foreign language rather than seeking out external opinions. However, both teachers and learners lack a general reading technique or strategy. Oftentimes, students undertake the reading task equipped with nothing more than a bilingual dictionary, a grammar book, and lots of courage. These efforts often end in frustration as the student builds mis-constructed nonsensical sentences after many hours spent on an aimless translation drill.

Consequently, we have decided to develop this series of interlinear translations intended to afford a comprehensive edition of unabridged texts. These texts are presented as they were originally written with no changes in word choice or order. As a result, we have a translated piece conveying the true meaning under every word from the original work. Our readers receive then two books in just one volume: the original version and its translation.

The reading task is no longer a laborious exercise of patiently decoding unclear and seemingly complex paragraphs. What's more, reading becomes an enjoyable and meaningful process of cultural, philosophical and linguistic learning. Independent learners can then acquire expressions and vocabulary while understanding pragmatic and socio-cultural dimensions of the target language by reading in it rather than reading about it.

Our proposal, however, does not claim to be a novelty. Interlinear translation is as old as the Spanish tongue, e.g. "glosses of [Saint] Emilianus", interlinear bibles in Old German, and of course James Hamilton's work in the 1800s. About the latter, we remind the readers, that as a revolutionary freethinker he promoted the publication of Greco-Roman classic works and further pieces in diverse languages. His effort, such as ours, sought to lighten the exhausting task of looking words up in large glossaries as an educational practice: "if there is any thing which fills reflecting men with melancholy and regret, it is the waste of mortal time, parental money, and puerile happiness, in the present method of pursuing Latin and Greek[2]".

Additionally, another influential figure in the same line of thought as Hamilton was John Locke. Locke was also the philosopher and translator of the Fabulae AEsopi in an interlinear plan. In 1600, he was already suggesting that interlinear texts, everyday communication, and use of the target language could be the most appropriate ways to achieve language learning:

> ...the true and genuine Way, and that which I would propose, not only as the easiest and best, wherein a Child might, without pains or Chiding, get a Language which others are wont to be whipt for at School six or seven Years together...[3]

---

1 "The journey is long through precepts, but brief and effective through examples". Seneca, Lucius Annaeus. (1961) Ad Lucilium Epistulae Morales, vol. I. London: W. Heinemann.

2 In: Hamilton, James (1829?) History, principles, practice and results of the Hamiltonian system, with answers to the Edinburgh and Westminster reviews; A lecture delivered at Liverpool; and instructions for the use of the books published on the system. Londres: W. Aylott and Co., 8, Pater Noster Row. p. 29.

3 In: Locke, John. (1693) Some thoughts concerning education. Londres: A. and J. Churchill. pp. 196-7.

Who can benefit from this edition?

We identify three kinds of readers, namely, those who take this work as a search tool, those who want to learn a language by reading authentic materials, and those attempting to read writers in their original language. The HypLern collection constitutes a very effective instrument for all of them.

1. For the first target audience, this edition represents a search tool to connect their mother tongue with that of the writer's. Therefore, they have the opportunity to read over an original literary work in an enriching and certain manner.
2. For the second group, reading every word or idiomatic expression in its actual context of use will yield a strong association between the form, the collocation, and the context. This will have a direct impact on long term learning of passive vocabulary, gradually building genuine reading ability in the original language. This book is an ideal companion not only to independent learners but also to those who take lessons with a teacher. At the same time, the continuous feeling of achievement produced during the process of reading original authors both stimulates and empowers the learner to study[1].
3. Finally, the third kind of reader will notice the same benefits as the previous ones. The proximity of a word and its translation in our interlinear texts is a step further from other collections, such as the Loeb Classical Library. Although their works might be considered the most famous in this genre, the presentation of texts on opposite pages hinders the immediate link between words and their semantic equivalence in our native tongue (or one we have a strong mastery of).

---

1 Some further ways of using the present work include:

1. As you progress through the stories, focus less on the lower line (the English translation). Instead, try to read through the upper line, staying in the foreign language as long as possible.
2. Even if you find glosses or explanatory footnotes about the mechanics of the language, you should make your own hypotheses on word formation and syntactical functions in a sentence. Feel confident about inferring your own language rules and test them progressively. You can also take notes concerning those idiomatic expressions or special language usage that calls your attention for later study.
3. As soon as you finish each text, check the reading in the original version (with no interlinear or parallel translation). This will fulfil the main goal of this

collection: bridging the gap between readers and original literary works, training them to read directly and independently.

Why interlinear?

Conventionally speaking, tiresome reading in tricky and exhausting circumstances has been the common definition of learning by texts. This collection offers a friendly reading format where the language is not a stumbling block anymore. Contrastively, our collection presents a language as a vehicle through which readers can attain and understand their authors' written ideas.

While learning to read, most people are urged to use the dictionary and distinguish words from multiple entries. We help readers skip this step by providing the proper translation based on the surrounding context. In so doing, readers have the chance to invest energy and time in understanding the text and learning vocabulary; they read quickly and easily like a skilled horseman cantering through a book.

Thereby we stress the fact that our proposal is not new at all. Others have tried the same before, coming up with evident and substantial outcomes. Certainly, we are not pioneers in designing interlinear texts. Nonetheless, we are nowadays the only, and doubtless, the best, in providing you with interlinear foreign language texts.

Handling instructions

Using this book is very easy. Each text should be read at least three times in order to explore the whole potential of the method. The first phase is devoted to comparing words in the foreign language to those in the mother tongue. This is to say, the upper line is contrasted to the lower line as the following example shows:

EL	SOMBRERO	DEL	REY	DE	TIBOTU
The	Hat	Of The	King	Of	Tibotu

The second phase of reading focuses on capturing the meaning and sense of the original text. As readers gain practice with the method, they should be able to focus on the target language without getting distracted by the translation. New users of the method, however, may find it helpful to cover the translated lines with a piece of paper as illustrated in the image below. Subsequently, they try to understand the meaning of every word, phrase, and entire sentences in the target language itself, drawing on the translation only when necessary. In this phase, the reader should resist the temptation to look at the translation for every word. In doing so, they will find that they are able to understand a good portion of the text by reading directly in the target language, without the crutch of the translation. This is the skill we are looking to train: the ability to read and understand native materials and enjoy them as native speakers do, that being, directly in the original language.

EL SOMBRERO DEL REY DE TIBOTU
The Hat

In the final phase, readers will be able to understand the meaning of the text when reading it without additional help. There may be some less common words and phrases which have not cemented themselves yet in the reader's brain, but the majority of the story should not pose any problems. If desired, the reader can use an SRS or some other memorization method to learning these straggling words.

EL SOMBRERO DEL REY DE TIBOTU

Above all, readers will not have to look every word up in a dictionary to read a text in the foreign language. This otherwise wasted time will be spent concentrating on their principal interest. These new readers will tackle authentic texts while learning their vocabulary and expressions to use in further communicative (written or oral) situations. This book is just one work from an overall series with the same purpose. It really helps those who are afraid of having "poor vocabulary" to feel confident about reading directly in the language. To all of them and to all of you, welcome to the amazing experience of living a foreign language!

Additional tools

Check out shop.hyplern.com or contact us at info@hyplern.com for free mp3s (if available) and free empty (untranslated) versions of the eBooks that we have on offer.

For some of the older eBooks and paperbacks we have Windows, iOS and Android apps available that, next to the interlinear format, allow for a pop-up format, where hovering over a word or clicking on it gives you its meaning. The apps also have any mp3s, if available, and integrated vocabulary practice.

Visit the site hyplern.com for the same functionality online. This is where we will be working non-stop to make all our material available in multiple formats, including audio where available, and vocabulary practice.

Table of Contents

Tristis Imago

TRISTIS IMAGO
Sad Imago

Hablábamos, mi amigo y yo, de cosas indiferentes
(We) spoke my friend and I of things careless

y triviales. El sol, próximo a desaparecer,
and trivial The sun close to disappear

arrojaba sobre la tierra una luz cálida y rojiza,
cast on the earth a light warm and reddish

y el bochorno que entraba por la abierta
and the sultry weather that entered through the open

ventana parecía esparcirse por
window seemed to spread itself through

todo el aposento. Las columnillas de humo de
all the chamber The little columns of smoke from
the whole chamber

nuestros cigarros subían hasta juntarse en
our cigars rose until to join themselves in

ligeras nubes que iban anidando en los casetones
light clouds that went nesting in the coffers

del artesonado, y el damasco que cubría las
of the paneling and the damask that covered the

paredes tomaba un tinte de color más rico que
walls took a shade of color more rich than

de costumbre.
-of- normal

La conversación empezó a languidecer, y
The conversation started to falter and

llegó un momento en que ambos
(there) arrived a moment in that (we) both

callamos, como si obedeciéramos algún
remained silent as if (we) obeyed some

misterioso mandato. Yo tenía cierto orgullo en
mysterious order I had certain pride on (for)

aquella estancia, en que reuniera todo lo que
that room in that (which) (I had) gathered all that what

poseía de mayor valor y más hondo afecto,
(I) possessed of large worth and more deep affection

y no era la primera vez que desde mi butaca
and not (it) was the first time that from my seat

paseaba la mirada sobre los muebles y cuadros
(I) passed the look over the furnitures and paintings

que la adornaban. Rafael también gustaba de
that her adorned Rafael also liked -of-
(it)

aquella colección y la elogiaba a menudo, de
that collection and her praised -at- often of
(it)

manera que no me sorprendió verlo recorrer
(a) manner that not me surprised to see him run over

con la vista aquel abigarrado conjunto de objetos.
with the sight that motley gathering of objects

Enfrente de donde nos hallábamos sentados, pendía
In front of where us (we) found seated hung

de la pared un retrato de busto de mi madre,
from the wall a portrait of (the) bust of my mother

ataviada según la moda del segundo Imperio.
dressed according to the fashion of the second Empire

A pesar de la luz que por momentos iba
At weight of the light that for moments went

apagándose, el retrato se destacaba muy bien,
to extinguish itself the portrait itself stood out very well

y se acentuaba en su rostro la inefable
and itself accentuated in her face the ineffable

dulzura que el pintor había sabido reproducir
sweetness that the painter had known to reproduce

fielmente.
faithfully

No sé cuánto tiempo permanecimos en
Not (I) know how much time (we) remained in

silencio. Repentinamente sentí una como ráfaga de
silence Suddenly (I) felt a like gust of

melancolía y dirigí la mirada hacia el retrato.
melancholy and directed the look at the portrait

5

Me estremecí al verlo, y noté que mi
Myself shook at the to see it and (I) noted that my
I shook at seeing it

amigo sufrió idéntica impresión.
friend suffered (an) identical impression

Nos miramos ambos, y él, poniéndose de pie,
Us (we) looked both and he setting himself of foot
We both looked standing up

dijo en voz muy baja:
said in (a) voice very low
(soft)

- ¡Está llorando!
(She) is crying

Yo asentí con la cabeza, y mi compañero con
I assented with the head and my companion with

paso quedo, salió de la estancia y cerró la
step held exited from the room and closed the
(restrained)

puerta tras sí, cuidadosamente.
door behind himself carefully

Entonces yo, presa de grande angustia, me
Then I taken of great anguish myself

acerqué al retrato y ví que se animaba. Una
approached to the portrait and saw that she moved A

nube de tristeza nubló el semblante de mi madre,
cloud of sadness clouded the likeness of my mother

y las lágrimas que brotaban de sus ojos cayeron
and the tears that sprung from her eyes fell

con mayor abundancia. Se movieron sus
with great abundance Themselves moved her

labios y oí una vez más la voz que veinte
lips and (I) heard one time more the voice that twenty

años enmudeciera.
years muted

- ¡Hijo mío! ¡Siento una gran piedad por ti! El
Son (of) mine (I) feel a great piety for you The

camino que tienes que recorrer es áspero y
road that (you) have to wander is rough and

difícil, y grandes sufrimientos serán tuyos. Por
difficult and great sufferings will be yours For

eso es que siento tan grande piedad por ti.

that (it) is that (I) feel such great piety for you

Nunca hagas a nadie partícipe de tus cuitas,

Never (you) make to no one participant of your worries

ni a tu mejor amigo; guárdalas siempre para ti.

nor to your best friend keep them always for you

Sé avaro de tus sentimientos; a nadie los digas.

Be greedy of your feelings to no one them tell

¡Hijo mío, cuánta piedad siento por ti!

Son (of) mine how much piety (I) feel for you

Las sombras de la noche penetraron casi

The shades of the night penetrated almost

repentinamente y pronto me envolvieron en

suddenly and soon me envolved in

densa obscuridad.

dense obscurity

Por fin, después de no corto espacio de tiempo,

By end after -of- no short space of time

At last (period)

encendí la luz y abrí la puerta. Rafael se
(I) lit the light and opened the door Rafael himself
(I turned on)

hallaba en la galería, en el hueco de una
found in the gallery in the gap of a

ventana, y al verme, pareció despertar de
window and at the to see me (he) seemed to wake up from
at seeing me

un sueño.
a dream

- ¡Rafael...! - exclamé; pero él me interrumpió,
Rafael (I) exclaimed but he me interrupted

diciendo:
saying

- ¡No me digas nada; no, ni a mí que soy
Not me tell nothing no nor to me that am
(not even)

tu mejor amigo!
your best friend

Y silenciosamente entramos de nuevo en el
And silently (we) entered of new in the

aposento. Con la luz artificial, las cosas todas
room With the light artificial the things all

presentaban su aspecto de costumbre, y el
presented their aspect of usual and the

retrato de mi madre la dulzura inefable de su
portrait of my mother the sweetness ineffable of her

rostro. Debajo de él, sobre una mesa, se hallaba
face Below of her on a table itself found

mi último soneto; lo tomé para leerlo a Rafael,
my last sonnet it (I) took for to read it to Rafael

y encontré que estaba humedecido y
and (I) found that (it) was moistened (wet) and

emborronado.
smudged

El Sombrero Del Rey De Tibotu

EL SOMBRERO DEL REY DE TIBOTU
The Hat Of The King Of Tibotu

El Rey de Tibotú tenía (naturalmente) tres hijos.
The King of Tibotu had naturally (of course) three sons

El mayor se llamaba Chapachapa, el segundo
The older (one) himself called Chapachapa the second

Chopochopo, y el menor Chipichipi. El rey
Chopochopo and the younger (one) Chipichipi The king

era muy rico: poseía diez y siete sombrillas
was very rich (he) possessed ten and seven seventeen umbrellas

de todos colores, un tapa-rabo verde y amarillo,
of all colors a covers-tail (loincloth) green and yellow

muy gracioso, y un sombrero alto, tan alto que
very gracious and a hat high so high that

rayaba en lo monumental. La reina, Sabihonda,
scratched on the monumental The queen Sabihonda
(verged)

usaba medias azules y era políglota: cuando
used stockings blue and was polyglot when
wore blue stockings

algo le caía muy en gracia, hablaba en chino,
something her fell much in grace (she) spoke in Chinese
she liked a lot

y cuando se enfadaba, gritaba en catalán.
and when herself (she) angered (she) shouted in Catalan
she got angry

El reino se componía, además de la populosa
The kingdom itself composed at more of the populous
(moreover)

ciudad de Tibotú, de dos islas. En una
city of Tibotu of two islands On one

se cosechaba gran cantidad de café y
itself harvested (a) great quantity of coffee and
was harvested

había numerosas vacas de ordeña; en la otra
had numerous cows of milking on the other
(there were)

se producía el cacao y había muy buenos
itself produced -the- cacao and had very good
was produced (there were)

panaderos y reposteros. Las islas eran
bakers and confectioners The islands were

vulgarmente conocidas por
in a vulgar way known for
(as)

"La-isla-de-café-con-leche", y
The-island-of-coffee-with-milk and

"La-isla-de-chocolate-con-bollos".
The-island-of-chocolate-with-buns

La familia real de Tibotú vivió feliz muchos años;
The family royal of Tibotu lived happily many years
royal family

pero una noche, el rey se comió, en la
but one night the king himself ate at -the-
ate up

cena, todo un lechoncillo al horno, y
dinner all a piglet at the oven and
a whole piglet (from the)

falleció a las pocas horas, rodeado de su mujer
passed away at the few hours surrounded of his wife
(wee) (by)

e hijos.
and sons

Transcurridos	los	nueve	minutos,	nueve	segundos,
(Having) passed	the	nine	minutes	nine	seconds

que	según	el	Ceremonial	de	aquella	Corte,
that	according to	the	Ceremony	of	that	Court

hay	que	esperar	antes	de	abrir	el	testamento
has	that	wait	before	-of-	to open	the	testament
one has to							(will)

del	monarca	fallecido,	se	encontró	que	la
of the	monarch	passed away	itself	found	that	the
			it was ascertained			

última	disposición	del	autócrata	era	que	su
last	disposition	of the	autocrat	was	that	his
	(will)					

populosa	ciudad	de	Tibotú	pasara	a	su	amada
populous	city	of	Tibotu	will pass	to	his	beloved

esposa,	y	las	islas	del	"Café-con-leche"	y
spouse	and	the	islands	of the	Coffee-with-milk	and

del	"Chocolate-con-bollos"	a	sus	dos	hijos,
of the	Chocolate-with-buns	to	his	two	sons

Chapachapa	y	Chopochopo,	respectivamente.	En
Chapachapa	and	Chopochopo	respectively	In

cuanto a Chipichipi, legábale su padre el
how much to Chipichipi bequeathed to him his father the

sombrero de copa.
hat of cup
top hat

Imagínese el júbilo de la cónyuge y de los
Imagine yourself the joy of the spouse and of the

hijos mayores, y el enfado del Benjamín de la
sons elder and the anger of the Benjamin of the
(youngest)

casa. ¿Para qué quería él un sombrero viejo, sucio
house For what wanted he a hat old dirty

y de forma tan poco artística?
and of form so little artistic

Invadió el ánimo del príncipe tal furia, que
Invaded the spirit of the prince such fury that
The spirit of the prince was invaded by

echó al suelo la despreciada prenda y
(he) threw at the floor the despised garment and

propinóle un fuerte puntapié. Pero al hacerlo,
gave it a strong point-to-foot But at the to do that
(kick) at doing that

sintió un agudo dolor en el pie, como si hubiese
(he) felt a sharp pain in the foot as if (he) had

chocado contra una piedra. Con mayor furia
hit against a stone With greater fury

todavía, tomó el sombrero y empezó a
still (he) took the hat and started to

despedazarlo con gran coraje, pero, he aquí, que
rip it to pieces with great courage but has here that
(spirit) (it was)

encontró, entre el forro y la copa, algo
(he) encountered between the cover and the cup something

duro, una piedra, efectivamente, más grande que
hard a stone in fact more large than

un huevo de gallina, aunque no tanto como uno
an egg of chicken although not so much like one

de avestruz; era roja como la sangra de un
of ostrich (it) was red like the blood of a

pichón y brillaba al sol de una manera
pigeon and shone at the sun of a way
in the sunlight (in)

sorprendente. Era nada menos que un rubí.
surprising (It) was nothing less than a ruby

No hay para qué referir la sensación que este
Not has for to recount the sensation that this
I shouldn't have to

hallazgo causó en todo el mundo. Baste decir que
discovery caused in all the world Enough to say that

todas las testas coronadas, y muchas que
all the heads crowned and many that
crowned heads

no lo eran, se disputaban la posesión de
not it were themselves disputed the possession of
not were crowned

tan magnífica joya. Los más interesados en
such (a) magnificent jewel The most interested in

obtenerla eran el Presidente de la República
to obtain it were the President of the Republic

Inglesa, el Gran Duque de Texcoco y Mr. Elihu
English the Great Duke of Texcoco and Mr Elihu

P Goggles, de Paradise, Texas. Inútil nos
P Goggles of Paradise Texas Useless to us
(Unnecessary)

parece decir que este último y célebre
(it) seems to say that this last (one) and famous

millonario fue quien adquirió la piedra preciosa,
millionaire was whom acquired the stone precious

pagando por ella diez y siete millones de dólares
paying for her ten and seven millions of dollars
(million)

en oro, y diez y siete en "Liberty Bonds", de
in gold and ten and seven in Liberty Bonds from

la décima séptima emisión, y haciéndose llamar,
the tenth seventh emission and making himself call
seventeenth (known)

de allí en adelante, "The Ruby King", o sea, "El
from there and ahead The Ruby King or be (it) The
(then)

Rey del Rubí".
King of the Ruby

Por supuesto, Chipichipi invirtió bien su dinero y
For supposed Chipichipi invested well his money and
Of course

se dio la gran vida. Compró un automóvil
himself gave the great life (He) bought an automobile

"Ford", un perro-policía, y un Diccionario de la
Ford a dog-police and a Dictionary from the
(police dog)

Academia. En cambio sus hermanos se
Academy In exchange his brothers themselves
However

arruinaron: el café se perdió, y las vacas de
ruined the coffee itself lost and the cows of
got lost

ordeña se murieron; el cacao bajó de
milking -themselves- died the cacao lowered of

precio y los panaderos y reposteros se
price and the bakers and confectioners themselves

declararon en perpetua huelga.
declared in perpetual strike

Y siempre que se hablaba del sombrero de
And always that itself talked of the hat of
(when) people talked

copa de su difunto esposo, exclamaba la Reina
cup of her passed away spouse exclaimed the Queen

Sabihonda, en portugués:
Sabihonda in Portuguese

19

"En todas las cosas, por despreciables que
In all the things for worthless that

parezcan, hay algo de valor, para el que
(they) seem has (there is) something of value for him that

sabe encontrarlo."
knows to find it

El Cofre

EL COFRE
The Chest

Las trémulas llamaradas, que el fuego de la
The trembling flames that the fire from the

chimenea despedía, hacían oscilar fantásticamente,
hearth released made fluctuate fantastically
caused to flicker

sobre las paredes del aposento, la sombra del
on the walls of the chamber the shadow of the

viejo don Alejandro. Arrebujado éste en un
old don Alejandro Wrapped up that (one) in an

sillón, al lado del ancho hogar, procuraba
armchair at the side of the wide fireplace (he) tried

calentar su cuerpo, entumecido, no tanto por el
to warm his body numbed not so much by the

mal tiempo que a la sazón hacía, cuanto por
bad weather that at the season (it) had how much for
(there was) (as)

los años y penas que sobre él pesaban. Pero,
the years and pains that on him weighted But

a pesar de su proximidad al fuego, sentía frío.
at weight of his proximity to the fire (he) felt cold
in spite

¡Cuántas noches pasara largas horas en el
How many nights passed long hours in the
(had he passed)

mismo sitio, fija la mirada en la rojiza lumbre!
same site fixed the gaze in the reddish light
(location)

A veces, los encendidos leños asumían formas que
At times the glowing logs assumed forms that
(took)

su imaginación trocaba en personas y
his imagination changed into persons and

sucedidos reales, y de esa manera convertía
happenings real and of that manner converted
actual events (in)

aquel hogar en escenario, en el cual se
that fireplace in (a) stage on the which itself

representaba a menudo el tétrico drama de su
presented -at- often the dismal drama of his

vida.
life

El primer acto, por decirlo así, era de escaso
The first act for to say it thus was of scarce

interés. Después de sus primeros años, pasados
interest After -of- his first years passed

al lado de su madre, veía su vida de colegio,
at the side of his mother (he) saw his life of (at) college

vida triste y sin amigos, que tanto influyó
life sad and without friends that so much influenced

sobre su carácter, haciéndolo huraño y retraído.
-on- his character making him shy and withdrawn

Empezaba el segundo acto con un cuadro
Started the second act with a painting

pavoroso. Sobre el lecho de muerte yacía su
dreadful On the bed of death lay his

madre, el único ser de él querido, y al
mother the only being of him beloved and at the

lado, de pie, contemplábala un hombre severo,
side of (at) (the) foot contemplated her a man strict

casi repugnante: su padre.
almost repugnant his father

Sucedíanse los demás actos del drama con toda
Occurred itself the more acts of the drama with all

fidelidad. Don Alejandro recorría las principales
fidelity (truthfulness) Don Alejandro roamed the main

capitales del mundo, en busca de distracción;
capitals of the world in search of distraction

pero todos huían de él, como si fuese un ser
but all fled from him as if (he) was a being

infecto: con lo cual se agriaba su carácter más
infected with the which itself soured his character more

y más. Cuando volvía a su casa, encontraba
and more When (he) returned to his house (he) found

que su padre se moría. Sin sentir dolor
that his father himself died Without to feel grief
was dying

alguno, veía cómo se apagaba la existencia
any (he) saw how itself extinguished the existence

del autor de sus días. El médico indicaba que
of the author of his days The medic indicated that

no había más recurso... Llegaba el sacerdote,
not had more recourse Arrived the priest
(there was) any help

pero el moribundo sólo lograba enunciar, con
but the dying only managed to enunciate with
(to utter)

gran dificultad, las palabras:
great difficulty the words

- ¡El cofre...!
The chest

El salón en que se hallaba don Alejandro
The salon in that itself located don Alejandro

guardaba muchas obras de arte y objetos
guarded many works of art and objects

antiguos. Entre ellos, en un rincón del aposento,
antique Between them in a corner of the chamber

se hallaba un gran cofre de hierro, cubierto,
itself found a large chest of iron covered
(was located)

casi en su totalidad, con clavos y remaches de
almost in its totality with nails and rivets of

bronce. Este era, sin duda alguna, el cofre al
bronze This was without doubt any the chest at the
any doubt

cual el moribundo había querido referirse, pero
which the dying had wanted to refer himself but

la llave no había podido encontrarse y el
the key not had been able to encounter itself and the
had not been found

secreto, si secreto había en él, permanecía
secret if (any) secret had in it remained
(there was)

ignorado.
unknown

Por milésima vez, don Alejandro dirigió la
For (the) thousandth time don Alejandro directed the

mirada hacia el ángulo de la estancia, y
gaze towards the corner of the room and

se extremeció al ver que el cofre se
-himself- shook at the to see that the chest itself
at seeing

hallaba abierto. La pesada tapa descansaba contra
found open The heavy lid rested against

el muro, dejando ver el vetusto y complicado
the wall letting see the ancient and complicated

mecanismo de su cerradura.
mechanism of its lock

Mucho tiempo permaneció el anciano sin
Much time remained the old man without

poder apartar de aquel sitio los espantados
to be able to part from that location the frightened

ojos. Por fin, haciendo un supremo esfuerzo,
eyes By end making a immense effort
At last

abandonó su sitial al lado de la chimenea, y
(he) left his seat at the side of the hearth and

con una sensación de espanto, se dirigió hacia
with a feeling of fear himself directed towards

el cofre. Al principio nada pudo distinguir
the chest At the beginning nothing (he) could distinguish

en el interior, pero pocos momentos después,
in the interior but (a) few moments after

vio un rectángulo amarillento que yacía en el
(he) saw a rectangle yellow that lay on the

fondo. Hincóse de rodillas y con mano trémula
bottom Sunk himself of knees and with hand trembling
He went down on his knees

extrajo aquel objeto. Era un sobre, manchado
extracted that object (It) was an envelope stained

por el transcurso del tiempo, sin rótulo de
by the passing of the time without label of

ninguna especie.
none sort
(any)

Repentino y formidable estrépito hízole volver
A sudden and formidable loud crash made him turn

el rostro amedrentado, y vio que la tapa
the face frightened and (he) saw that the lid

del cofre había caído en su sitio, cerrándolo
of the chest had fallen in its place closing it

de nuevo.
of new
again

Volvió al lado del hogar, para leer el
(He) returned to the side of the fireplace for to read the

contenido del sobre: pero sus manos estaban de
content of the envelope but his hands were of

tal manera temblorosas, que no pudo
such manner trembling that not (he) could

verificarlo. Después de algunos instantes,
verify it After -of- some instants
(moments)

logró conquistar relativa tranquilidad;
(he) managed to conquer (a) relative calmness
(to regain)

abrió la cubierta y con ojos de terror,
(he) opened the cover and with eyes of terror

extrajo el pliego que contenía. Pero le daba
extracted the folder (folded sheet) that (it) contained But it gave

vueltas la cabeza, y tuvo que apoyarse en
turns the head and (he) had that (to) support himself on

la butaca para no caer al suelo. Fijó
the seat for not to fall to the floor (He) focused

de nuevo la vista en el fuego del hogar, y vio
of new again the sight on the fire of the hearth and saw

claramente la pavorosa escena de la muerte de
clearly the frightening scene of the death of

su madre. Anonadado, miró el anciano
his mother Overwhelmed watched the old man

furtivamente a su alrededor, temiendo ser
furtively at his surroundings fearing to be

observado, y decidió hacer un esfuerzo para
observed and decided to make an effort for

leer el pliego; pero el papel se escapó de
to read the folder (folded sheet) but the paper itself escaped from

sus temblorosas manos y cayó entre las llamas
his trembling hands and fell between the flames

que lo consumieron vorazmente.
that it consumed voraciously

Don Alejandro miró hacia el rincón en donde
Don Alejandro watched towards the corner -in- where

estaba el cerrado cofre y se acercó más
was the closed chest and himself approached more

aún a la chimenea, pero, a pesar de su
still to the hearth but at weight of his

proximidad al fuego sentía frío.
proximity to the fire (he) felt cold

Un Hombre Practico

UN HOMBRE PRACTICO
A Man Practical

El Padre Ministro de la Casa de Novicios de la
The Father Minister of the House of Novices of the

Compañía de Jesús en Espadal era pequeñín, de
Company of Jesus in Espadal was very small of

rostro colorado, cabello blanco y expresión
face colored hair white and expression

risueña. Decíase que en su juventud tuvo trato
smiling (It) was said that in his youth (he) had (a) deal

con las Musas, pero si tal fue el caso, ningún
with the Muses but if such was the case no

resabio de ello adivinábase en el Padre Hurtado.
aftertaste of that guessed itself (could be guessed) in the Father Hurtado

El Padre Ministro, varón santo si los hay, era
The Father Minister male saint if them has was
there are any

ante todo un hombre práctico; pruebas de
before everything a man practical proves of

serlo dio en mil ocasiones, al grado
to be that (he) gave in (a) thousand occasions at the degree

de hacerse esta cualidad suya proverbial, no
of to make himself that quality (of) his proverbial not

sólo entre la comunidad, sino en toda la
only between the community but in all the

comarca. Inútil nos parece decir que aquel
region Useless us (it) seems to say that that

establecimiento marchaba admirablemente, como
establishment marched admirably as
(ran)

cuadraba a la gran Institución de que formaba
squared to the great Institution of what (it) formed
(suited)

parte.
part

Una alegre mañana de junio, en que el Padre
One cheerful morning of June in that the Father

Ministro comprobaba con satisfacción que el
Minister ascertained with satisfaction that the

consumo de patatas en el mes pasado había
consumption of potatoes in the month passed had

sido mucho menor que el del correspondiente
been much less than that of the corresponding (month)

del año anterior, un leve toque en su puerta
from the year before a light knock on his door

vino a interrumpir su tarea.
came to interrupt his task

- ¡Adelante! - exclamó.
Ahead (Come in) (he) exclaimed

El Hermano Fuente dio vuelta al picaporte y
The Brother Fuente gave turn to the latch and

dijo:
said

- Padre Ministro; un hombre desea hablarle.
Father Minister a man desires to talk to you

El Padre Hurtado, enemigo de antesalas, frunció
The Father Hurtado enemy of anterooms frowned

ligeramente el entrecejo, pero contestó;
lightly the between-eyebrows but answered

- Que pase.
That (he) passes
(he enters)

Pocos momentos después, se presentaba un
(A) Few moments after himself presented an

individuo, cuya descripción es ocioso hacer, pues
individual whose description is idly to make because
(useless)

era como miles otros: de cuarenta años,
(he) was as thousands (of) others -of- forty years

poco más o menos, sano al parecer, y pobre,
little more or less sane at the to seem and poor
seemingly healthy

puesto que el dinero, según reza el refrán,
set that the money according to prays the refrain

no
not

puede estar disimulado.
can be hidden

- Buenos días, Padre.
Good days Father

- Buenos nos los dé Dios. ¿Qué se ofrece?
Good (things) us them gives God What itself (you) offer

- Padre Hurtado, vengo a ver a usted porque
Father Hurtado (I) come to see -to- you because

me encuentro en situación difícil. No tengo
myself (I) find in (a) situation difficult Not (I) have

qué comer. Desde que paró la fábrica....
what (anything) to eat Since that stopped the factory

- Si os metéis en huelgas, - interrumpió el
If yourself (you) put in strikes interrupted the

religioso.
religious (one)

- No podía yo nada en contra, y tuve que
Not could I (do) nothing -in- against (it) and had that (to)

hacer lo que todos los compañeros. El caso es
do that what all the companions (did) The case is

que el trabajo no se reanuda ni lleva trazas de
that the work not itself resumes nor carries traces of

serlo. Me muero de hambre, y aunque a
to be that Myself (I) die of hunger and although to

Dios gracias, no tengo nadie que dependa de mí,
God thanks not (I) have no one that depends of me

necesito trabajar. Conozco algo de
(I) need to work (Do you) know something of

jardinería....
gardening

- Amigo, - dijo el Padre Hurtado, - en esta casa
Friend said the Padre Hurtado in this house

no tenemos jardín.
not (we) have (a) garden

- He trabajado como albañil.
(I) have worked as builder

- En esta casa, gracias a Dios, no hay
In this house thanks to God not has
(there are)

reparaciones ni obras que hacer por el momento.
reparations nor works that do for the moment
(to)

- Padre, yo le ruego, yo le suplico que me
Father I you ask I you beg that me

proporcione algo. Usted que es un hombre tan
(you) give something You that are a man so

práctico....
practical

Hay que advertir que todo este tiempo, el Padre
Has that warn that all this time the Father
(to)

Hurtado casi no había reparado en su
Hurtado almost not had glanced on his

interlocutor, pues mientras sostenía el diálogo,
questioner since while (he) held the dialogue

seguía haciendo números; pero al notar un
(he) continued doing numbers but at the to note a
(counting) when noticing

leve acento de amargura o de reproche en la
light accent of bitterness or of reproach in the

última frase del obrero, alzó la vista y lo
last phrase of the worker (he) raised the view and him

miró fijamente por algunos instantes.
watched fixedly for some instants

- Repito, - prosiguió, - que no tengo trabajo que
(I) repeat (he) continued that not (I) have work that (to)

proporcionarle en esta casa. Pero si quiere usted
give you in this house But if want you

acudir a nuestro Colegio en Carrión de la Vega,
come to our College in Carrion of the Vega

estoy seguro que su Rector, el Padre Rodríguez,
(I) am sure that its Rector the Father Rodriguez

le dará todo lo que le haga falta.
you will give all that what you makes lack need

- Padre, mil gracias, - replicó el hombre. -
Father (a) thousand thanks replied the man

He confesado y comulgado esta mañana, y
(I) have confessed and done communion this morning and

estaba seguro de que usted me sacaría de
(I) was sure of that you me would get out of

apuros. Juan González le será siempre
troubles Juan Gonzalez you will be forever

agradecido. ¿Quisiera usted darme, Padre Ministro,
thankful Want you give me Father Minister

una carta o papel de recomendación?
a letter or paper of recommendation

El Padre Hurtado tomó una cuartilla, la partió
The Father Hurtado took a sheet it divided

cuidadosamente en dos, guardando una mitad para
carefully in two keeping a half for

uso futuro, y trazó en el papel breves
use future and traced (wrote) on the paper (some) short

renglones. La metió dentro de un sobre, lo cerró
lines It put inside of an envelope it closed

y dirigió, y lo entregó a Juan González.
and directed (addressed) and it handed over to Juan Gonzalez

Despidióse éste, y al abrir la
(He) dismissed himself (of) that (one) and at the to open (at opening) the

puerta para marcharse, lo detuvo el Padre
door for to march himself (to set off) him stopped the Father

Hurtado diciéndole:
Hurtado telling him

- Espere un momento, hermano.
Wait a moment brother

Abandonó su escritorio, mojó dos dedos en una
(He) abandoned his study wetted two fingers in a

pila de agua bendita que colgaba en la pared, y
basin of water blessed that hung on the wall and

tocó con ellos la mano del obrero, diciéndole
touched with them the hand of the worker telling him

cariñosamente;
lovingly

- ¡Vaya con Dios!
Go with God

El Rector de Carrión de la Vega abrió
The Rector of Carrion of the Vega opened

cuidadosamente el sobre que acababa de
carefully the envelope that finished of

entregarle el portero, y extrajo la misiva
to hand over to him the worker and extracted the missive

del Padre Hurtado; la leyó, y sin alzar la
of the Father Hurtado it (he) read and without to raise the

cabeza, miró al Hermano por encima de sus
head looked at the Brother -by- over -of- his

espejuelos.
lenses
(glasses)

- No entiendo esto, - dijo. - ¿Quién ha traído
Not (I) understand this (he) said Whom has brought

este papel?
this paper

- Un hombre a quien no conozco. Parece
A man -to- whom not (I) know (He) seems

obrero.
(a) worker

- ¿No trae ningún mensaje de palabra?
Not (he) brings none message of word
(any) oral message

- Nada me ha dicho, Padre.
Nothing me has (he) said Father

- ¿En dónde está este hombre?
In where is this man

- Espera en la portería.
(He) waits at the door

- Voy a verle.
(I) go to see him

Ligeramente contrariado, el corpulento Padre
Slightly annoyed the corpulent Father

Rodríguez se levantó trabajosamente de su
Rodriguez himself raised with a lot of work from his

asiento, no sin dirigir la mirada al cúmulo
seat not without to direct the look at the stack

de cartas que había sobre el escritorio esperando
of letters that (he) had on the desk awaiting

contestación, y se encaminó a la portería.
answer and himself walked to the gatehouse

- Buenas tardes.
Good afternoon

- Buenas tardes, Padre, - contestó Juan González,
Good afternoon Father answered Juan Gonzalez

con el rostro iluminado por la esperanza.
with the face illuminated by the hope

- ¿Usted ha traído este billete del Padre
You have brought this note from the Father

Hurtado?
Hurtado

- Sí, Señor.
Yes Sir

- Y ¿nada le indicó que me
And nothing to you (he) indicated that me

dijera de palabra?
(you) said of word
should tell me

- Nada, Padre.
Nothing Father

- Es raro. Haga favor de esperar un
(That) is strange Do (me a) favor of to wait (for) a

momento.
moment

El Rector estaba sorprendido. Que un hombre
The Rector was surprised That a man

como el Padre Hurtado hubiera escrito esas
like the Father Hurtado would have written those

cuantas palabras, tan faltas de sentido común, era
how many words so lacking of sense common was

un absurdo. En las galerías inmediatas a la
-an- absurd In the galleries close to the

portería encontró al Padre Procurador y
gatehouse (he) encountered -to the- Father Proctor and

al Primer Prefecto, quienes, al ver a su
to the First Prefect who at the to see -to- their
at seeing

superior, levantaron sus birretes respetuosamente.
superior raised their caps respectfully

- El Padre Hurtado se ha vuelto loco, - dijo
The Father Hurtado himself has turned mad said

el Rector sin más preámbulo.
the Rector without more preamble
(introduction)

- ¡Imposible! - exclamaron a un tiempo los otros
Impossible exclaimed at one time the other

dos.
two

- Entonces, ¿cómo explican ustedes que me
Then how explain you that me

envíe este billete? - preguntó, y alargó el
(he) sends this note (he) asked and handed over the

papel al Prefecto, quien leyó en voz alta los
paper to the Prefect who read in voice high the

siguientes renglones:
following short lines

- "Estimado Padre Rodríguez: Le ruego se sirva
Estimated Father Rodriguez I ask itself serves

dar cristiana sepultura al portador de la
to give (a) Christian burial to the carrier of the

presente. Su afmo. Hermano en Xto.
present Your very affectionate {afectísimo} Brother in Christ {Cristo}

Alonso Hurtado, S.J."
Alonso Hurtado S.J.

Hubo un silencio. El Padre Ministro de Espadal,
Had (There was) a silence The Father Ministro of Espadal

tenido por el hombre más cuerdo de la Provincia
held for the man most sane of the Province

no podía haber escrito esas palabras.
not could have written those words

Instintivamente, los tres religiosos se
Instinctively the three religious persons themselves

dirigieron a la portería para interrogar a Juan
directed to the gatehouse for to interrogate -to- Juan

González, seguros de que se trataba de una
Gonzalez certain -of- that itself (it) dealt of (with) a

broma.
joke

Pero Juan González, yacía en el suelo, boca
But Juan Gonzalez lay on the ground mouth (face)

arriba, con los ojos muy abiertos. Dos hilos de
up with the eyes very open Two strains of

sangre negra manchaban su labio superior, y
blood black tainted his lip upper and

tenía la mano izquierda crispada contra el
(he) had the hand left cramped against the

pecho.
breast

Similia Similibus

SIMILIA SIMILIBUS
Like like
{similia remedia similibus malis; same remedy for same problem}

Como ya murió el célebre homeópata Dr.
As already (has) died the famous homeopath Dr

Idiáquez, puedo divulgar el secreto que me
Idiaquez (I) can divulge the secret that me

impuso bajo mi palabra.
(he) imposed under my word
I swore not to tell

Hace precisamente diez años que principió la
(It) does precisely ten years -that- began the
(Since)

extraña dolencia que motivó mi visita a aquel
strange illness that motivated my visit to that

facultativo, y cuya rápida curación fue el primer
physician and which rapid healing was the first
the rapid healing of which

escalón de su fama. Desde pequeño fui
step of his fame From small (I) was

enfermizo y débil, por lo cual puedo decir,
infirm and weak for the which (I) can say

sin gran exageración, que toda mi niñez y
without great exaggeration that all my childhood and

la mitad de mi juventud las pasé en
the half of my youth them passed in

consultorios de doctores. En verdad, era una
consults of (with) doctors In reality (it) was a

maravilla para todos mis allegados que fuese yo
miracle for all my relatives that was I

viviendo. Apenas cumplí los treinta años, empecé
living Hardly (I) fulfilled (reached I) the thirty years started (I)

a sufrir los más agudos dolores de cabeza que
to suffer the most sharp pains of head that

puedan imaginarse, los cuales de día en día
(you) can imagine yourself the which from day in day

aumentaban al grado de hacerme la vida un
augmented at the degree of to make me the life a

verdadero martirio. Solamente descansaba yo de
true torture Only rested I from

ellos cuando dormía, razón por la cual procuré
them when (I) slept reason for the which (I) tried

cortejar a Morfeo incesantemente.
to woo to Morpheus incessantly

Pero llegó el día en que ni aún el sueño pudo
But arrived the day in that not even the sleep could

ahuyentar mis sufrimientos; y lo más extraño
chase away my sufferings and the most strange

del caso era que, a medida que soñaba las
of the case was that at measure that (I) dreamed the
as

cosas más fantásticas y hermosas, más agudos
things most fantastic and beautiful more sharp

eran los dolores que me torturaban. Se
were the pains that me tortured Yourself

comprenderá, por lo tanto, que entonces quise
will understand for that much that then (I) wanted

huir del sueño, apurando fuertes dosis de café:
to flee from the sleep draining strong doses of coffee

y esperaba yo la muerte como una ansiada
and awaited I the death like an longed for

liberación. Más, a pesar de todos mis esfuerzos
liberation More at weight of all my efforts
in spite

para permanecer despierto y del horror con
to remain awake and from the horror with

que veía yo llegar la noche, me vencía al fin
that saw I arrive the night me overcame at the end

el sueño, y en seguida presentábanse a mi
the sleep and in followed presented themselves to my
subsequently

mente las más peregrinas visiones que puedan
mind the most sacred visions that (you) can

imaginarse, aun en ese mundo inexplicable.
imagine yourself even in that world inexplicable

Lluvias de estrellas, caleidoscópicas auroras,
Rains of stars kaleidoscopic auroras

extrañas floraciones, embargaban mi mente
strange flowerings charged my mind

de continuo; a veces, sobre un mar fosforescente
of continuous at times over a sea phosphorescent
continuously

veía yo navegar hacia mí un galeón de oro con
saw I navigate towards me a galleon of gold with

velamen de carmín y grana, mientras
sail of carmine and cochineal while
{red from insect}

indescriptible armonía sonaba en mis oídos. Y
(an) indescribable harmony sounded in my ears And

a medida, repito, que aquellas visiones eran más
at measure (I) repeat that those visions were more
at the level

hermosas, más agudo era el dolor que
beautiful more sharp was the pain that

atormentaba mi cerebro. Y tal terror se
tormented my brain And such terror itself

posesionó de mi alma, que no comprendo cómo
possessed of my soul that not (I) understand how

no fui a parar a un manicomio.
not went to end at an asylum

Ninguno de los facultativos que consulté
none of the physicians that (I) consulted

encontraba remedio a mi mal, y no puse
found (a) remedy to my illness and not put

término a mis días con mi propia mano, gracias a
end to my days with my own hand thanks to

mis principios religiosos. Por fin, siguiendo el
my principles religious By end following the
At last

consejo de no recuerdo qué médico famoso,
advise of not (I) remember what medic famous

determiné que varios de los doctores más
(I) determined that various of the doctors most

eminentes de la ciudad se reunieran en
eminent of the city themselves gathered in

consulta, y después de dos horas del más
consult and after of two hours of the most

penoso interrogatorio, pronunciaron mi sentencia.
painful examination pronounced my sentence

Mi mal era incurable y degeneraría en locura;
My illness was incurable and would degenerate in madness

el tumor que se había formado en mi cerebro
the tumor that itself had formed in my brain

era inoperable y la muerte se aproximaba,
was inoperable and -the- death itself approached

aunque lentamente.
although slowly

Salí de aquel consultorio como un hombre
(I) exited from that consulting room like a man

beodo. He dicho que muchas veces había
drunk (I) have said that many times (I) had

deseado la muerte, y sin embargo, aquel día
desired -the- death and without obstacle that day
nevertheless

amaba yo la vida, a pesar de mis horribles
loved I the life at weight of my horrible
in spite

sufrimientos. Embargada mi mente, como debe
sufferings Loaded my mind as (it) must
(Being depressed)

suponerse, caminé hacia mi casa por calles
be assumed (I) walked towards my house by streets

apartadas, temeroso de encontrar alguna persona
remote fearful of to encounter some person

conocida. Repentinamente, no sé qué impulso
known Suddenly not (I) know what impulse
(familiar)

hizo fijar mi vista en una pequeña placa de metal
made fix my view in a small plaque of metal
(focus)

sobre la puerta de una sucia habitación. Leí el
on the door of a filthy dwelling (I) read the

letrero: "Dr. Idiáquez, homeópata", y casi sin
sign Dr Idiaquez homeopath and almost without

pensar en lo que hacía, penetré en la casa y
to think in it what (I) did (I) entered in the house and

subí la destartalada escalera.
went up the ramshackle stair(s)

El Dr. Idiáquez era un hombre vulgar y
The Dr Idiaquez was a man vulgar and

demacrado, y su consultorio una guardilla sucia
emaciated and his consulting office a attic filthy

y miserable. Ambos me recordaron, enseguida, la
and miserable Both me reminded in following the

escena del boticario en "Romeo y Julieta".
scene of the apothecary in Romeo and Juliet

Expuse mi mal y la opinión de los facultativos
(I) exposed my illness and the opinion of the medics
(I laid out)

a quienes consultara, y el Dr. Idiáquez me
-at- whom (I) consulted and -the- Dr Idiaquez (to) me

escuchó con la mayor atención.
listened with the greatest attention

- La enfermedad de usted, - me dijo al fin,
The disease of you me (he) said at the end

- es extraña, indudablemente, y proviene en
is strange undoubtedly and comes forth in

efecto de un tumor que se ha formado en su
fact from a tumor that itself has formed in your

cerebro; pero no sólo no es incurable, sino que
brain but not only not (it) is incurable but that

puedo librarlo de ella en tres días.
(I) can free you of her (it) in three days

- ¡Cómo! - exclamé, - no queriendo creer lo
How (I) exclaimed not wanting to believe that

que escuchaba.
what (I) heard

- Sencillamente, - respondió con mucha calma. -
Simple (he) answered with much calm

Aquí tiene usted estos glóbulos que tomará usted
Here have you these drops that will take you

cada tres horas: tres del frasco marcado A. y
each three hours three from the vial marked A. and

cuatro del marcado B., alternativamente. Hoy
four from that marked B. alternately Today

es lunes; el viernes próximo vendrá usted a
(it) is Monday the Friday next will come you to

verme, ya curado.
see me already cured

Pagué su modesto honorario, y bajé la
(I) paid his modest fee and went down the

escalera rápidamente, como si volara en alas de
stair(s) quickly as if (I) will fly on wings of

la esperanza. La tarde estaba tibia y
the hope The afternoon was warm and

perfumada, y la puesta del sol parecía un
scented and the setting of the sun seemed a

incendio en los montes lejanos.
fire in the mountains distant

Aquella noche, por primera vez, me abandonaron
That night for (the) first time me abandoned (left alone)

mis sufrimientos, pero los bellos sueños también
my sufferings but the beautiful dreams also

huyeron, y fui atormentado por horribles
fled and (I) was tormented by horrible

pesadillas. Estas aumentaron a tal grado en las
nightmares These augmented to such degree in the

dos noches siguientes, que puedo asegurar que
two nights following that (I) can assure that

ni el Dante pudiera imaginárselas en lo
neither -the- Dante could imagine himself them in the

más profundo del Averno.
most deep of the Averno

Por fin llegó el ansiado viernes, y
By end arrived the anxiously awaited Friday and
At last

efectivamente, libre de todo sufrimiento físico y
effectively free of all suffering physical and

moral, subí la destartalada escalera que
moral (I) went up the ramshackle stair(s) that

conducía al consultorio del Dr. Idiáquez.
conducted (led) to the consulting office of -the- Dr Idiaquez

Éste me recibió afablemente, y me aseguró
This (one) me received affably and me assured

que mi curación era definitiva. Ese día compré un
that my cure was definitive That day (I) bought a

busto de Hahnmann y lo coloqué en lugar
bust of Hahnmann and it placed in (a) place

prominente de mi biblioteca.
prominent of my library

Inútil me parece decir que la noticia de mi
Useless to me (it) seems to say that the news of my

rápida curación se extendió por todo el
rapid cure itself extended through all the

país, y el nombre del Dr. Idiáquez
country and the D of -the- Dr Idiaquez

en seguida se hizo célebre. De allí en adelante,
in followed subsequently itself made famous From there in forward

efectuó las
(he) effected the

más sorprendentes curaciones, y al cabo de
most surprising cures and at the end of

poco tiempo, reunió una fortuna considerable.
little time (he) gathered a fortune considerable

Lo que más intrigaba a sus pacientes era que
That what most intrigued -to- his patients was that

jamás recetaba, sino que él mismo
never (he) prescribed but that he himself

proporcionaba las medicinas, marcándolas
proportioned the medicines marking them

generalmente con letras, aunque a veces también
generally with letters although at times also

con números.
with numbers

Naturalmente, contraje con él vínculos de
Naturally (I) contracted with him links of

estrecha amistad y lo visitaba a menudo en
tight friendship and him (I) visited -at- often in

su nueva y lujosa casa. Un día me atreví a
his new and luxurious house One day myself dared to

decirle:
tell him

- Doctor, hace mucho tiempo que he querido
Doctor (it) did (since) much time that have wanted

hacerle una pregunta.
to make you (to ask you) a question

- ¿Cuál es?
Which is

- ¿De qué se componían los glóbulos que me
From what itself composed the drops that me

proporcionaron mi maravillosa curación?
proportioned my wondrous cure

- Amigo mío, ese es mi secreto; pero puesto
Friend (of) mine that is my secret but set

que a usted le debo mi fortuna, se lo diré, si
that to you it (I) owe my fortune itself it will say if

me promete, si me jura, no decirlo
me (you) promise yourself if me (you) swear not to tell it

mientras yo viva. En cuanto muera, queda usted
while I live (am alive) In how much (I) day remain you

en libertad para proclamarlo a los cuatro vientos.
at liberty for to proclaim it to the four winds

Hice la promesa requerida, y con una sonrisa
(I) made the promise required and with a smile

muy triste, nunca he visto en la cara de un
very sad never have (I) seen in the face of a

hombre una sonrisa más triste, dijo el Dr.
man a smile more sad said -the- Dr

Idiáquez lentamente:
Idiaquez slowly

- Los glóbulos marcados "A" se componían
The drops marked A themselves composed

de agua y azúcar; los marcados "B" de azúcar
of water and sugar those marked B of sugar

y agua.
and water

El Reportazgo

EL REPORTAZGO
The Reportage

Comprendo que ustedes, los reporteros, tengan
Understanding that you the reporters have

deberes para con sus lectores y que,
duties -for- with your readers and that

por lo tanto, anden siempre a caza de noticias;
for that so much (you) go always at hunt of notices
therefore (news)

pero, como soy enemigo de repeticiones, quiero
but as (I) am enemy of repetitions (I) want

que el diario que usted representa, por ser el
that the newspaper that you represent for to be that

de mayor importancia en el país, sea mi único
of greatest importance in the country be my only

portavoz en este asunto. Dentro de diez minutos
mouthpiece in this case Inside of ten minutes

llegará mi mujer; mientras tanto, pues, le suplico
will arrive my wife while as much then you (I) beg

que escuche con atención y escriba a mi
that (you) listen with attention and write at my

dictado. Yo le daré todos los pormenores del
dictation (speech) I you will give all the details of the

caso, que como verá, es cosa bien sencilla.
case that as (you) will see is (a) thing quite simple

Empezaré por decirle que contaba yo muy
(I) will start by to tell you (telling you) that counted I I was very

pocos años de edad, cuando murió mi padre,
few years of age young when died my father

legándome una fortuna cuantiosa. Pero como
bequeathing to me a fortune substantial substantial fortune But as

el ocio nunca entró en mis cálculos, decidí
the leisure never enters in my counts (I) decided

estudiar una carrera, y elegí la carrera de
to study a career and chose the career of

médico-cirujano. Aquí, entre nos, le confesaré
medic-surgeon Here between us you (I) confess

que siempre he considerado la medicina como
that always (I) have considered the medicin like

la carabina de Ambrosio, pero la cirugía, ¡ah! eso
the carbine of Ambrosio but the surgery Ah that
the fake carbine of a famous robber

es otra cosa. Por medio de la cirugía pueden
is (an)other thing by means of the surgery (the) can

curarse radicalmente todas las dolencias de la
cure radically all the ails of -the-

humanidad, y no está lejano el día en que hasta
humanity and not (it) is far the day in that up to

la misma muerte pueda evitarse por su medio.
the same (very) death can be evited by its means

Mis profesores se quedaron asombrados de
My professors themselves were remained surprised of (by)

la extraordinaria pericia que adquirí desde un
the extraordinary expertise that (I) adquired from a

principio: el bisturí en mis manos era como el
beginning the scalpel in my hands was like the

pincel en las de un artista. Cada corte mío
paintbrush in those of an artist Each cut (of) mine

era una maravilla de precisión y de arte, sí
was a wonder of precision and of art yes

señor, de arte. Gané los primeros premios en la
sir of art (I) gained the first prizes in the
(I won)

Academia, y cuando se me expidió el título
Academy and when itself (to) me (was) issued the title

de Cirujano, se hizo constar en él que jamás
of Surgeon itself made conclude in this that never

se habían obtenido calificaciones más altas.
themselves had obtained qualifications more high
were received

La primera operación de importancia que ejecuté,
The first operation of importance that (I) executed

después de haber sido recibido, fue la amputación
after of to have been received was the amputation

de ambas manos del célebre pianista Gerolstein.
of both hands of the famous pianist Gerolstein

Por supuesto que era absolutamente innecesario
For supposed that (it) was absolutely unnecessary
Of course

que dicho señor perdiera las dos manos, pero
that said sir lost the two hands but

como no me gustaba nada su manera de
as not me (it) pleased nothing his manner of

interpretar Beethoven, decidí cortar el mal de
to interpret Beethoven (I) decided to cut the evil of
(by the)

raíz; y perdóneme esta ligera "plaisanterie".
root and pardon me this light joke
{french}

Por aquel tiempo conocí a Matilde. No recuerdo
By that time (I) knew -to- Matilde Not (I) remember

si fue en un baile en el palacio de la Princesa
if (it) was in a dance in the palace of the Princess

Dorodinski, o si fue en las carreras de caballos.
Dorodinski or if (it) was in the courses of (the) horses

Pero sí tengo muy presente que desde el
But indeed (I) have very present that from the
(clear)

primer momento que la ví, comprendí que
first moment that her (I) saw (I) understood that

era la mujer más hermosa que ha habido en
(she) was the woman most beautiful that has had in
there was

el mundo, y por lo tanto, que tenía que ser
the world and for that as much that (she) had to be
accordingly

mi esposa. Yo era entonces excesivamente
my wife I was then excessively

romántico; no le llamará la atención saber que
romantic not you (I) will call the attention to know that
(on the fact)

toda mi corte fue hecha a la luz de la luna. La
all my cut was made at the light of the moon The

orquesta del Conservatorio tocaba todas las
orchestra of the Conservatory played all the

noches música selecta debajo de su ventana, y
nights music selective under of her window and
(certain)

hasta llegué a pagar a un poeta de fama para
up to (I) arrived to pay -to- a poet of fame for

que le escribiera madrigales, que yo firmaba.
that her (he) wrote madrigals that I signed
(short poems)

Para no hacer largo este relato, le diré que
For not to make long this tale you (I) will say that

mientras se llevaban a cabo los preparativos
while themselves carried to end the preparations

de nuestra boda, Matilde no hacía más que llorar,
of our wedding Matilde not did more than cry

llorar... Lloraba de amor por mí, según me
cry (She) cried of love for me according to me

aseguró su madre... Matilde, he dicho, es y
assured her mother Matilde (I) have said is and

será la mujer más hermosa de la tierra. Pero,
will be the woman most beautiful of the earth But

amigo mío, bien dice el refrán que no hay
friend (of) mine well says the proverb that not has (there is)

dicha completa en este mundo. Poco tiempo
happiness complete in this world Little time

después de nuestro matrimonio, una terrible
after of our matrimony a terrible

sospecha empezó a martirizarme. Matilde fue
suspicion started to torture me Matilde was

desde un principio una esposa modelo; pero los
from a beginning a wife model exemplary wife but the

besos apasionados que yo le daba jamás eran
kisses passionate that I her gave never were

correspondidos; jamás posaba su mirada sobre mí
answered never set (she) her look on me

con cariño, y todos los pequeños sacrificios que
with love and all the little sacrifices that

por ella hacía ni siquiera eran notados, mucho
for here (I) made not (for) certain were noticed much

menos agradecidos... En fin, llegó el día
less appreciated In (the) end (there) arrived the day

amargo en que la sospecha se tornó en certeza.
bitter in that the suspicion itself turned in certainty

Con pretexto de sentirme cansado y apoyar mi
With pretext of to feel myself tired and support (rest) my

cabeza sobre su pecho, hice el terrible
head on her breast (I) made the terrible

descubrimiento de que Matilde, la mujer más
discovery of that Matilde the woman most

hermosa de la tierra, "no tenía corazón". Mucho
beautiful of the earth not had (a) heart Much

tiempo permanecí anonadado; pero súbitamente un
time (I) remained overwhelmed but immediately a

rayo de luz iluminó mi mente.
ray of light illuminated my mind

Casi todos los días acudía yo al anfiteatro de
Almost all the days arrived I at the amphitheater of

la Academia y presenciaba los cursos.
the academy and (I) was present at the courses

Recordé que, en la mañana de aquel día,
(I) remembered that in the morning of that day

se había recogido en la calle el cadáver de una
itself had collected in the street the corpse of a
there was

joven del bajo pueblo que había sido
young woman from the lower people that had been
(common)

atropellada por un tranvía. Tendría la misma edad,
run over by a tram-way (She) had the same age
(streetcar)

más o menos, que Matilde.
more or less than Matilde
(as)

Eran las diez de la noche, cuando me presenté
Were the ten of the night when myself (I) presented
It was ten o'clock at night

al conserje de la Academia y le pedí las
to the concierge of the Academy and him asked (for) the

llaves del anfiteatro para recoger unos
keys of the amphitheater for to grab some

instrumentos que había yo dejado olvidados. El
instruments that had I left forgotten The

conserje me las franqueó en seguida y hasta
concierge me them passed them in followed and until
subsequently (also)

ofreció acompañarme, pero yo le dispensé esa
offered to accompany me but I him dispensed (of) that

molestia, y penetré solo en el salón. Un cuarto
trouble and entered alone in the salon A quarter

de hora después salía de allí llevando en la
of hour after (I) exited from there carrying in the

mano un estuche que mostré al conserje, para
hand a case that (I) showed to the concierge for

que viera que efectivamente era de mi
that (he) saw that effectively (it) was of my

propiedad, y en el fondo de la bolsa de mi
property and in the bottom of the pocket of my

abrigo un bulto pequeñísimo, envuelto en gasa. Eso
coat a bump very small enveloped in gauze That

naturalmente no lo vio el buen hombre.
of course not him saw the good man

Matilde estaba ya en su lecho, cuando fui a
Matilde was already in her bed when (I) went to

darle las buenas noches. Noté que se
give her the good nights (I) noticed that she
(wish her) good night

estremeció un poco al verme entrar en su
shuddered a bit at the to see me enter in her
at seeing me

alcoba; pero yo la tranquilicé con una sonrisa, y
bedroom but I her calmed down with a smile and

me acerqué a besar su casta frente. Todo lo
myself approached to kiss her chaste front All that
(forehead)

tenía yo hábilmente preparado, y fue cuestión
had I skillfully prepared and (it) was (a) question

de medio segundo aplicarle el cloroformo y
of half (a) second to apply to her the chloroform and

adormecerla. Una vez logrado esto, pude
to let her sleep One time succeeded that (I) could

proseguir mi tarea con toda calma. En realidad, la
proceed my task with all calm In reality the

operación fue sencillísima: se redujo a abrirle el
operation was very simple itself reduced to open her the
only was needed

pecho y colocar en el sitio correspondiente el
breast and locate in the site corresponding the

corazón de la joven. Y aquí debo consignar
heart of the young woman And here (I) must state

una cosa extraordinaria. Apenas había yo
a thing extraordinary Hardly had I

comenzado la operación, cuando aparecieron sobre
started the operation when appeared on

las sábanas dos o tres rosas rojas, que fueron
the sheets two or three roses red that were

multiplicándose, hasta cubrir casi todo el lecho.
multiplying themselves until to cover almost all the bed

El éxito de la operación, no por previsto dejó
The success of the operation not for foreseen left
unexpectedly

de satisfacerme; al contrario, con el mayor
of to satisfy me at the contrary with the greatest

gusto del mundo, me senté al lado de mi
pleasure of the world myself sat down at the side of my

mujer esperando que despertara de su sueño. Su
wife waiting that (she) woke up from her sleep Her

nuevo corazón latía tan regularmente, que
new heart beat so regularly that

cualquiera hubiera creído que era el tic-tac
anyone had believed that (it) was the tic-toc

del reloj que se hallaba sobre la
of the clock that itself located on the

mesa de noche... Hasta mucho después del
table of night Until much after of the
nightstand

amanecer permanecí allí, admirando la peregrina
dawning remained (I) there admiring the sacred

belleza de mi mujer, que se destacaba
beauty of my wife that herself stood out
(who)

espléndidamente sobre su lecho de rosas rojas.
splendidly on her bed of roses red

No sé qué hora sería, cuando entró la
Not (I) know what hour (it) was when entered the

doncella en la alcoba. Como es una mujer muy
maid in the bedroom As (it) is a woman very

lista, en seguida comprendió el prodigio y
smart in followed (she) understood the prodigy and

salió de la estancia dando gritos de
(she) exited from the room giving shouts of

admiración. Pocos momentos después, llegaron los
wonder Few moments after arrived the

hermanos de Matilde y muchas otras personas.
brothers of Matilde and many other persons

Por más que hice para hacerlos comprender que
For more that (I) did for to make them understand that

la operación que había yo llevado a cabo era en
the operation that had I carried to end was in

realidad muy sencilla, se obstinaron en
reality very easy themselves insisted in

traerme, casi a la fuerza, a este palacio, en
to bring me almost at the force to this palace in

donde tienen su morada los hombres más
where keep their dwelling the men most

eminentes de la tierra... En efecto, vea usted:
eminent of the earth In fact see you

aquel caballero del sombrero alto y la corbata
that gentleman of the (with the) hat high and the necktie

amarilla es el Gran Khan de la China; el otro,
yellow is the Great Khan of the China the other

que se pasea con las manos detrás de la
that himself passes with the hands behind of the

espalda, es López, el famoso ingeniero López,
shoulder is Lopez the famous engineer Lopez

quien logró construir el puente entre la tierra
who managed to construct the bridge between the earth

y el sol, obra reputada durante mucho tiempo
and the sun work deemed during much time

como impracticable. El que está leyendo el
as impracticable Who that is reading the

periódico y tiene los zapatos rotos es el
newspaper and has the shoes broken is the

Emperador y Autócrata de todas las Américas, y
Emperor and Autocrat of all the America's and

aquel anciano a su lado que se mece la
that elderly man at his side that himself swings the

barba, ese es, !ah! no me atrevo a decir a usted
beard that is ah not me (I) dare to say to you

quién es. Pero me ha prometido que en
whom (it) is But me (he) has promised that in

cuanto llegue mi mujer y se arroje en mis
how much arrives my wife and herself throws in my

brazos, formidable estruendo rasgará las nubes,
arms formidable thundering will tear (open) the clouds

y una bandada de alados serafines bajará
and a band of winged seraphs will come down

para llevarnos, a Matilde y a mí, al paraíso.
to take us to Matilde and to me to the paradise

La Puerta De Bronce

LA PUERTA DE BRONCE
The Gate Of Bronze

Sentado en un amplio sillón de velludo carmesí,
Seated in a broad seat of velvet crimson

al lado de ancha ventana, el Cardenal de
at the side of (a) wide window the Cardinal of

Portinaris estaba dictando su testamento. A la
Portinaris was dictating his testament At the

primera cláusula que contenía su profesión de Fe,
first clause that contained his profession of Faith

había logrado dar un giro distinto del
(he) had succeeded to give a turn distinct of the

acostumbrado, de manera que a la par de un
accustomed (usual) of way that at the level of a

compendio de la Religión Católica resultaba
compendium of the Religion Catholic (it) resulted (to be)

un verdadero opúsculo literario. El Prelado, muy
a true opus literary The Prelate very

satisfecho, prosiguió a enumerar cada uno de sus
satisfied continued to enumerate each one of his

bienes, y al hacerlo, parecía que iban
goods and at the to do that (it) seemed that (they) went

arrancándose las más hermosas páginas de la
tearing themselves the most beautiful paginas from the

historia del arte. El notario escribía a toda prisa
history of the art The notary wrote at all haste

y, a pesar de estar muy acostumbrado a ese
and at weight of to be very accustomed to that

género de trabajos, se fatigaba en grado sumo,
kind of work himself tired in grade top
very much

y gruesas gotas de sudor aparecían sobre su
and thick drops of sweat appeared on his

calva frente.
bald forehead

Terminadas las cláusulas preliminares, el Cardenal
Terminated the clauses preliminary the Cardinal
(When finished)

hizo una pausa y dirigió la mirada vagamente
made a pause and directed the gaze vaguely
paused

a través de la ventana de su estudio. La Plaza
-to- through -of- the window of his study The Square

del Duque era un hervidero de gente, y el
of the Duke was a boiler of people and the
(swarm)

Prelado seguía con la vista el ir y venir de
Prelate followed with the view the go and come of

carruajes y peatones. Transcurrió algún espacio
coaches and pedestrians (There) passed some space

de tiempo; el notario se pasó el pañuelo por
of time the notary himself passed the kerchief for

la frente varias veces, y por fin observó
the front various times and at last observed
(forehead)

tímidamente:
timidly

- ¿Sí, Eminencia?
Yes (Your) Eminence

Pero el Cardenal permanecía callado.
But the Cardinal remained silent

- ¿Si, Eminencia? - insinuó de nuevo el letrado.
Yes (Your) Eminence insinuated of new the lawyer
(hinted) again

La verdad era que el Cardenal Diácono de la
The truth was that the Cardinal Deacon of the

Basílica de Santa María de las Rosas estaba
Basilisk of Santa Maria of the Roses was

perplejo; no encontraba a quién nombrar heredero.
perplex not (he) found to whom to name (as) heir

Miembro de una de las más esclarecidas familias
Member of one of the most famous families

de Toscana, con él terminaba su ilustre
of Toscana with him terminated his illustrious

progenie: su único sobrino, el Conde Fabricio de
progeny his only nephew the Count Fabricio of

Portinaris, se había marchado a América hacía
Partinaris himself had marched to America since
had gone

quince años y no se había vuelto a tener
fifteen years and not itself had returned to have

noticia de él. Ministros diplomáticos y
notice from him Ministers diplomatic and
Diplomatic ministers

agentes consulares, por más averiguaciones
agents consular for more verifications
consular agents no matter how many

que hicieran, no habían podido proporcionar
that (they) made not (they) had been able to proportionate
(to acquire)

ningún informe, y todo el mundo consideraba
none information and all the world considered
(any)

que el Conde había muerto. Desde sus primeros
that the Count had died Since his first

años, don Fabricio había dado pruebas de un
years don Fabricio had given proves of a

carácter indomable, su bolsillo fue siempre un
character indomitable his pocket was always a

pozo sin fondo, y no era secreto para nadie
hole without bottom and not (it) was secret for no one

que sus locuras habían conducido a su madre a
that his lunacies had lead -to- his mother to

un sepulcro prematuro.
a grave premature
(early)

Los ojos del Cardenal se empañaron de
The eyes of the Cardinal themselves blurred from

lágrimas y durante largo tiempo estuvo pensando
tears and during (a) long time (he) was thinking

a quién nombrar heredero. Sabía que las
to whom to name heir (He) knew that the
(of)

llamadas obras de beneficencia poco podrían
called works of charity little would be able
(mentioned)

aprovecharse de una fortuna que consistía
to take advantage themselves of a fortune that consisted

más bien en objetos de arte que en bienes
more well in objects of art than in goods
(of)

materiales, y dolíale el alma al pensar que
material and hurt him the sould to the to think that
at thinking

éstos fueran a parar a manos del anónimo e
these were to end up at (the) hands of the anonymous and

insípido personaje que se llama el Estado.
insipid personage that itself named the State

Decidió por fin legar todo su caudal a algún
(He) decided by end to bequeath all his wealth to a
at last

amigo, y resolvió hacerlo a favor del Príncipe
friend and resolved to do it to favor of the Prince

de Sant' Andrea, prócer bondadoso y magnánimo
of Sant Andrea hero kind and magnanimous

Mecenas.
patron

- Instituyo por mi único y universal heredero, -
(I) institute for my only and universal heir

empezaba a dictar el Cardenal, cuando sonó
started to dictate the Cardinal when sounded

leve toque en una puerta.
light knock(ing) on a door

- ¡Adelante! - exclamó el Prelado, y apareció
Forward exclaimed the Prelate and (there) appeared
(Come in)

en el umbral un sirviente vestido de negro.
on the threshold a servant dressed of black
(in)

Adelantóse éste y presentó en una salvilla
Forwarded himself this one and presented on a salver
He came forward

de plata una tarjeta, que el Príncipe de la Iglesia
of silver a card that the Prince of the Church

tomó con cierto gesto de enfado. Si al leer
took with certain gesture of anger If at the to read
at reading

en ella: "El Conde Fabricio de Portinaris"
on her The Count Fabricio of Portinaris
it

experimentó alguna sorpresa, pudo dominarla
(he) experienced some surprise (he) could dominate her
(control it)

en seguida, pues con tono tranquilo dijo al
in following then with tone calm said to the
following it

notario:
notary

- Ramponelli, mañana terminaremos.
Ramponelli tomorrow (we) will finish

Puede Vd. retirarse.
Can you retire yourself
You can go

El notario recogió sus papeles, metiólos dentro de
The notary gathered his papers put them inside of

un cartapacio, y con este bajó el brazo, fue a
a satchel and with this under the arm went to

besar el anillo cardenalicio, y salió de la
kiss the ring cardinalic and exited from the

estancia después de hacer profunda reverencia.
room after -of- to make (a) deep reverence
(bow)

En seguida ordenó a su camarero:
In following ordered to his chamberman

- ¡Que pase el Conde!
That pass the Count

Don Fabricio de Portinaris rayaba en los
Don Fabricio of Portinaris scratched (neared) in the

cincuenta años. Era extraordinariamente delgado
fifty years (He) Was extraordinary thin

y bajo de cuerpo; tenía la nariz aguileña, el
and low of body (small) (he) had the nose eagle-like the

cabello entrecano y el rostro tan lleno de
hair grizzled and the face so full of

arrugas, que a primera vista aparecía estar
wrinkles that at first sight (he) appeared to be

sonriendo continuamente.
smiling continually

Al verlo entrar en el estudio, su tío ni
At the to see him (At seeing him) enter in the study his uncle neighter

se inmutó ni se puso de pie: sólo dijo
himself moved nor himself put of (on) foot only said

secamente, dirigiendo involuntaria mirada al
dryly directing involuntarily (the) look at the

retrato de César Borgia que pendía en uno de los
painting of Cesar Borgia that hung on one of the

muros.
walls

- No esperaba veros más, sobrino. Creí que
Not awaited to see you more nephew (I) believed that

habíais muerto.
(you) had died

- Aún vivo, Eminencia, - repuso el Conde
Still alive (your) Eminence

sonriendo, e hizo ademán de besar la mano del

Prelado, pero éste la retiró disimuladamente
surreptitiously

indicando con ella una butaca cercana. Tomó
indicating with her a seat close Took

asiento el Conde, y después de unos instantes
(a) seat the Count and after -of- some instants

de embarazoso silencio, dijo:
of embarassing silence (he) said

- He llegado esta mañana, y creí de mi
Has arrived this morning and (I) believed of my

deber, antes que nada, saludar a vuestra
duty before that nothing salute to our
than anything

Eminencia.
Eminence

- Os lo agradezco, - contestó el Cardenal,
You it (I) thank for answered the Cardinal

tomando polvos de su tabaquera de oro. - Y,
taking dusts from his tabacco box of gold And

decidme, - prosiguió, - ¿encontrásteis en el
tell me (he) continued did you find in the

Nuevo Mundo todas aquellas cosas que aquí
New World all those things that here

echábais de menos? ¿Aquella libertad, aquella
threw of less That freedom that
missed

cuantiosa fortuna, aquella igualdad encantadora
large fortune that equality enchanting

entre los hombres, aquella (aquí sonrió el
between the men that here smiled the

Cardenal) verdadera democracia?
Cardinal true democracy

- Encontré en el Nuevo Mundo, Eminencia,
(I) encountered in the New World (your) Eminence

lo mismo que en Europa. Quince años he
the same that/(as) in Europe Fifteen years (I) have

vivido una vida angustiosa, y hoy vengo a
lived a life anguished and today (I) come to

impetrar vuestro perdón y a morir en mi
obtain by asking your pardon and to die in my

país.
country

Fue tal su acento de sinceridad, que el
(It) Was such his accent of sincerity that the

Cardenal se puso de pie solemnemente y
Cardinal himself set of foot solemnly and
(on)

bendijo a don Fabricio de Portinaris. Era la hora
blessed -to- don Fabricio of Portinaris Was the hour

del ocaso y los rayos del sol que se ponía
of the sunset and the rays of the sun that itself set

hacían más intensa la roja vestidura del prócer.
made more intense the red dress of the hero

Al principio el regreso del Conde fue
At the beginning the return of the Count was

escasamente comentado en la Ciudad, porque
scarcely discussed in the City because

había casi, desaparecido su memoria. Pero pronto
had almost disappeared his memory But soon

volvió a hablarse de él, porque el Cardenal de
returned to talk itself of him because the Cardinal of

Portinaris, a pesar de su robusta salud y no
Portinaris at weight of his robust health and not
in spite

avanzada edad, decaía notablemente, y un mes
advanced age decayed notably and a month

después se hallaba al borde del sepulcro.
after himself found at the edge of the grave

No faltó quien hablase en voz baja de
Not (there) lacked (people) who talked in voice low of

sutiles venenos traídos de América y alguien
subtle poisons brought from America and someone

recordó, en plena tertulia, que los Portinaris
remembered in plain social gathering that the Portinaris

descendían de Cesar Borgia.
descended from Cesar Borgia

Al fallecer el Prelado y abrirse su
At the to die the Prelate and to open itself his
When the prelate died

testamento, se supo que había legado todos
testament itself knew that had bequeathed all

sus bienes a Don Fabricio.
his goods to Don Fabricio

El nuevo Príncipe se ausentó enseguida de
The new prince himself absented next from

la Capital, y estableció su residencia en una
the Capital and established his residence in a

"villa" cercana, en donde llevó una vida retirada
villa close by in where (he) led a life retired

y tranquila. A las pocas personas con quienes
and calm To the few persons with whom

trataba, refería que estaba escribiendo sus
(he) dealt refered that (he) was writing his

memorias.
memories

Pero pasados algunos meses, decidió regresar a
But passed (after) some months (he) decided to return to

la Corte y allí se dijo que pensaba dar
the Court and there himself said that (he) thought to give

grandes recepciones en su palacio, pues deseaba
great receptions in his palace then desired

contraer matrimonio y llevar la vida que
to contract matrimony and lead the life that

correspondía a su clase.
corresponded to his class

No viene al caso hacer una reseña del
Not (it) comes to the case to make a review of the
It is not necessary

Palacio de Portinaris, porque ha sido descrito
Palace of Portinaris because (it) has been described

mil veces. En toda obra referente al Arte
(a) thousand times In all work refering to the Art

del Renacimiento ocupa preferente lugar, y
of the Renaissance (it) occupies (a) preferential place and

es conocidísimo aún de las personas que jamás
(it) is well known even of the persons that never
(by)

han visitado la Ciudad Ducal. Baste recordar que,
have visited the City Ducal Enough to remind that

entre las innumerables obras de arte que
between the innumerable works of art that

encierra, quizá sea la más notable la hermosa
(it) enclosed maybe was the most notable the beautiful

reja de entrada, labrada en bronce con tal
grid of entrance carved in bronze with such

maestría, que todos están acordes con
artistry that all were accorded with

atribuirla al autor de las puertas del
to attribute them to the author of the doors of the

bautisterio florentino. En los tableros inferiores
baptism from florence In the panels lower

se destaca, en alto relieve, la historia de aquel
itself highlighted in high relief the history of that

Hugo de Portinaris que, después de defender
Hugo of Portinaris that after of to defend

heroicamente la fortaleza del Borgo, fue
heroically the fortress of the Borgo was

degollado, junto con su mujer y sus dos
beheaded together with his wife and his two

hijas, por el victorioso y sanguinario Orlando
daughters by the victorious and bloody Orlando

Testaferrata. Gruesos, pero exquisitamente labrados,
Testaferrata Thick but exquisitely worked

barrotes abalaustrados sostienen el medio punto
bars balustraded support the half point

que la remata, en cuyo centro campea
that it topped off in which center championed

orgullosamente, la puerta que constituye las
proudly the gate that constitutes the

armas parlantes de la familia, mientras que
weapons speaking of the family while that

coronas, tiaras, espadas y llaves cruzadas,
crowns tiaras swords and keys crossed

pregonan por doquier los grandes honores que
preached -for- everywhere the great honors that

ésta ha gozado desde tiempo inmemorial.
it has enjoyed since time immemorial

Llegó el Príncipe a su palacio con las primeras
Arrived the Prince to his palace with the first

sombras de la noche. Al ascender la escalera
shadows of the night At the to ascend the stair(s)
At ascending

de honor, sintió un desmayo y hubiera caído
of honor (he) felt a swoon and would have fallen

al suelo, si no se apoyara en el pedestal de
to the floor if not himself supported on the pedestal of

una estatua, que decoraba el primer descanso.
a statue that decorated the first landing

Repúsose enseguida, y atravesó con paso
(He) set back himself next and traversed with step
(He got back up)

rápido la larga galería del Poniente, seguido de
fast the large galery of the Poniente followed of
(West) (by)

su mayordomo, y entró en la cámara,
his majordomo and entered in the chamber

llamada del Papa Calixto, que había sido
called of the Papa Calixto that had been
named after the

dispuesta para su dormitorio. Era amplísima y,
arranged to his bedroom (It) was wide and
(as)

a diferencia de las demás estancias del palacio,
at difference of the more rooms of the palace
(other)

relativamente sobria. Pocos pero ricos muebles la
relatively sober Few but rich furniture it
(simple) (expensive)

exornaban y el techo carecía de "plafond"
decorated and the roof lacked of ceiling

alegórico, motivo por el cual el Príncipe la
allegoric reason for the which the Prince it

prefirió a las demás, pues, como dijo sonriendo
preferred to the others since as (he) said smiling

al mayordomo, no quería estar viendo los
to the majordomo not wanted to be seeing the
he did not want

ángeles y mujeres desnudas de Julio Romano
angels and women naked of Julio Romano

desde su lecho.
from his bed

Aquella noche, don Fabricio tomó ligerísima
That night don Fabricio took (a) very light

comida, y después se instaló en su gabinete,
meal and after himself installed in his cabinet

a escribir, hasta hora muy avanzada. El vasto
to write until (an) hour much advanced (later) The vast

edificio estaba sumido en el más profundo
building was submitted in the most deep

silencio, pues toda la servidumbre se había
silence since all the servitude itself had

retirado a descansar, y sólo podía oírse el
retired to rest and only could hear itself the

rasguear de la pluma sobre el papel. Larga fue
scratching of the feather over the paper Long was

la carta que escribió el Príncipe, y bastante
the letter that wrote the prince and quite some

tiempo	tomó	en	leerla	y	hacerle	algunas
time	(he) took	in	to read it	and	to make it	some

correcciones.	Por	fin	la	dobló	cuidadosamente,
corrections	By	end	it	(he) folded	carefully
	At last				

y	después	de	haberla	metido	dentro	de	un
and	after	of	to have it	put	inside	-of-	an

sobre	grande,	la	dirigió	a	una	persona	de
envelope	large	it	directed	to	a	person	of

vulgar	apellido,	residente	en	la	República	del
vulgar	name	resident	in	the	Republic	of the
(commoner)						

Pánuco.	Se	disponía	a	lacrarla	y	sellarla,
Panuco	Himself	arranged	to	lacquer it	and	seal it

cuando	se	dibujó	en	su	rostro	una	expresión	de
when	itself	painted	on	his	face	an	expression	of

sorpresa	y	de	miedo.	El	gabinete	se	hallaba
surprise	and	of	fear	The	cabinet	itself	found

contiguo	al	estudio	que	había	sido	del
next	to the	study	that	had	been	of the

Cardenal, y al alzar el Príncipe la cabeza en
Cardinal and at the get up the Prince the head in

busca del sello, notó que por debajo de la
search of the seal (he) noted that -for- under -of- the

puerta de comunicación con aquella estancia, se
door of communication with that room itself

veía una brillante raya de luz.
saw a shining ray of light

Don Fabricio, pasados algunos instantes de
Don Fabricio (when) passed some instances of

sobresalto, logró dominarse y hasta sonreír;
surprise managed to control himself and until smile

y levantóse de su asiento para ir a apagar
and rising himself from his seat for to go to turn off

la luz, que inadvertidamente habría dejado algún
the light that inadvertently had left some

criado encendida en el estudio. Abrió la
servant lit in the study (He) opened the

puerta resueltamente, ... y ¡se heló su sangre!
door resolvedly and itself froze his blood

Sentada en el sillón, con su tabaquera abierta en
Seated in the armchair with his tobacco box open on

la mano derecha, y los dedos de la izquierda
the hand right and the fingers of the left

en ademán de tomar unos polvos, hallábase la
in (a) gesture of to take a powder found himself (was located) the

prócer figura del Cardenal de Portinaris.
illustrious person of the Cardinal of Portinaris

- No esperaba veros más, - dijo
Not (I) awaited to see you (any) more (he) said

lentamente. - Creí que habíais muerto, sobrino.
slowly (I) thought that (you) had died nephew

Presa del mayor terror, don Fabricio huyó,
Caught by the greatest terror don Fabricio fled

llamando en alta voz al mayordomo y otros
calling in loud voice -to- the majordomo and other

sirvientes; pero nadie acudía en su auxilio, y
servants but no one arrived in his aid and

recorrió las galerías dando voces que
(he) ran around the galleries giving (uttering) voices (words) that

retumbaban en las bóvedas de la señorial
reverberated in the arches of the lordly

mansión.
mansion

- ¡Antonio, Bernardo, Julio, Gilberto! - gritaba,
Antonio Bernardo Julio Gilberto (he) shouted

pero nadie quería contestar, y con verdadero
but no one wanted to answer and with true

pavor bajó, puede decirse que rodó, la
dread lowered (he) could tell himself that rolled the

escalera, y corrió a llamar al conserje.
stairs and ran to call to the concierge

Grandes golpes dio en su puerta con ambas
Great bangs (he) gave on his door with both

manos, pero nadie oía sus desesperadas voces de
hands but no one heard his desperate voices of (words)

terror.
terror

Acercóse a la entrada de palacio y
(He) approached himself to the entrance of (the) palace and

quiso abrir la puerta de bronce que la cerraba;
wanted to open the gate of bronze that it closed

pero por más esfuerzos que hizo, no pudo
but for more attempts that (he) made not (he) could

lograr moverla un milímetro, y por fin, en su
manage to move it a milimeter and at last in his

desesperación, concibió la idea de salir por
desperation (he) conceived the idea of to go out -for-

entre los barrotes, pues a toda costa quería
between the bars since at all cost (he) wanted

abandonar aquella casa. Como hemos dicho, don
to abandon that house As (we) have said don

Fabricio era extremadamente delgado, y decidió
Fabricio was extremely thin and (he) decided

intentar pasar el cuerpo por aquella parte de
to try to pass the body through that part of

la reja, en que los barrotes eran más esbeltos y,
the grill in that the bars were most slim and

por consiguiente, había mayor espacio entre ellos.
as consequence had more space between them

A la madrugada siguiente, enorme concurso
At the early morning next (an) enormous competition (jostling mass)

de curiosos se aglomeraba a la
of curious onlookers themselves agglomerated (gathered) at the

entrada del palacio. La cabeza del Príncipe,
entrance of the palace The head of the Prince

amoratada y descompuesta, se hallaba presa
turned blue and decomposed itself found caught

entre dos barrotes, y los ojos,
between two bars and the eyes

saltándosele de las órbitas, parecían
popping themselves of him from the orbits (eye sockets) seemed

mirar con terror el tablero, en el cual Ghiberti
to watch with terror the panel in the which Ghiberti

había cincelado magistralmente la degollación de
had chiselled magistrally the beheading of

Hugo de Portinaris por el despiadado Orlando
Hugo of Portinaris by the merciless (ruthless) Orlando

Testaferrata.
Testaferrata

Los Jugadores De Ajedrez

LOS JUGADORES DE AJEDREZ
The Players Of Chess

I
I

Angustias, india tarasca de raza pura, era maestra
Angustias native Tarasca of race pure was master
Tarascan native pure race

en el difícil arte de cuidar y entretener a
in the difficult art of to take care and to entertain -to-

los niños. Durante varios años sirvió en mi
the children During various years (she) served in my

familia, prodigando sus cuidados, sucesivamente, a
family lavishing her cares successively on

los cinco hermanos que éramos. Si nuestra casa
the five brothers that (we) were If our house

era visitada por alguna enfermedad, Angustias se
was visited by some disease Angustias herself

hallaba siempre a la cabecera de la cama, y
found always at the head of the room and

cuando se trataba de enjugar lágrimas,
when itself dealt of to wipe tears

consecuencia de alguna travesura de chiquillos, su
consequence of some antic of kids her

palabra cariñosa nos proporcionaba pronto
word tender us proportioned soon
tender words (gave)

consuelo. Pero la ciencia de la bondadosa niñera
consolation But the science of the kind nanny

era más patente cuando estábamos contentos.
was more patent when (we) were happy
(obvious)

Inventando juegos nuevos, haciendo gestos
Inventing games new making gestures
new games

verdaderamente estrambóticos, gracias a sus nada
(that were) truly outlandish thanks to her not

clásicas facciones, o contando cuentos jamás
classic features or telling stories never

imaginados, nos hacía gratísimas las horas del
imagined to us made very gratifying the hours of the

atardecer y, llegada la hora, sabía
sunset and (when) arrived the hour (she) knew

conducirnos suavemente al mundo de los
to lead us gently to the world of the

sueños. Otro don particular de Angustias era la
dreams (An)other gift particular of Angustias was the

pronta contestación que daba a las numerosas
immediate answer that (she) gave to the numerous

y peregrinas preguntas que solía hacerle la
and wide ranging questions that used to make her the

gente menuda. Era tal la espontaneidad de la
people small Was such the spontaneity of the
children Such was

respuesta y tan grande el aplomo con que la
response and so great the aplomb with that she

daba, que jamás pusimos en tela de juicio la
gave (it) that never (we) set in cloth of mind the
in question

solución por ella propuesta a cualquier problema
solution by her proposed to some problem

que se presentaba a nuestros infantiles cerebros.
that itself presented to our childish brains

Los recuerdos de mi infancia están estrechamente
The memories of my infancy were directly

ligados con la Hacienda de San Isidro Labrador,
tied with the Estate of Saint Isidor Farmer

en donde residíamos la mayor parte del año. La
in where (we) resided the largest part of the year The

finca, cercana a la ciudad de México, fue
estate close to the city of Mexico was

propiedad de la Compañía de Jesús desde los
property of the Company of Jesus from the

tiempos más remotos de la Colonia, y cuando
times most remote of the Colony and when

los célebres religiosos fueron expulsados de los
the famous religious ones were banished from the

dominios españoles, por las razones que Carlos
dominions Spanish for the reasons that Charles
Spanish dominions

III tuvo a bien guardar "en su real pecho",
(the) Third had to well guard in his real breast

fue adquirida por un mi antepasado.
was aquired by a my ancestor
an ancestor of mine

Se comprenderá, pues, que la casa de la
Itself will understand then that the house of the
It will be understood

Hacienda tenía más carácter de monasterio que
Estate had more (the) character of (a) monastery than

de finca de campo, y mi padre,
of (an) estate of (the) countryside and my father

siguiendo el ejemplo de sus mayores, quiso que
following the example of his elders wanted that

conservara siempre el austero aspecto que desde
(it) conserved always the austere aspect that from

un principio tuvo. Las estancias, todas abovedadas
a beginning (it) had The residences all vaulted

y de poca elevación; los interminables claustros
and of small altitude the interminable cloisters

con arquería de medio punto; los muros, gruesos
with arcade of half point the walls thick

como los de un castillo medioeval; y
like those of a castle medieval and
medieval castle

principalmente la comarca toda ayuna de encantos
mainly the region all fast of enchanting
(lacking)

naturales, - pues ostentaba, como únicas galas,
naturals — since (it) displayed like unique finery
(environs)

extensos magueyales y uno que otro eucalipto
extensive agaves and one that other eucalyptus
(or)

en medio de los campos de maíz y de cebada,
in half -of- the fields of maize and of barley
between

- hacían de la Hacienda de San Isidro
— (they) made from the Estate of Saint Isidor

Labrador un sitio que a muchos repugnaba, pero
Farmer a site that to many disgusted but

que a otros, al contrario, atraía por su misma
that to others at the contrary attracted for his own

desnudez y severidad. Inútil me parece decir
nakedness and severity Useless to me (it) seems to say

que para nosotros era un verdadero
that for us (it) was a true

"buen retiro"; en aquellos tiempos todavía se
well retired in those times already themselves
good retirement

conservaban muchas de las costumbres del
(they) conserved many of the habits of the

Virreinato, y mi padre era para los peones y
Vice-royalty and my father was for the laborers and

sirvientes, más que el amo a quien se debía
servants more than the master to whom itself (was) owed

respeto, el jefe de una dilatada familia.
respect the chief of an expanded family

La capilla era quizá la estancia más interesante
The chapel was maybe the residence most interesting

de la Hacienda. No era amplia, pero ostentaba
of the Estate Not (it) was wide but displayed

enorme retablo de madera dorada, al estilo
(an) enormous altarpiece of wood gilded at the style

de churriguerra, zócalo de azulejos, y pavimento
of Churriguerra plinth of tiles and pavement

de mármol en losetas blancas y negras,
of marble in tiles white and black

alternadas. Lo que más me llamaba la atención
alternating That what most me called the attention

eran los sepulcros de mis antepasados. Empotrados
were the sepulchres of my ancestors Embedded

en ambas paredes laterales del presbiterio,
in both walls lateral of the presbytery

hallábanse los nichos cubiertos con sendas
were found themselves the niches covered with two

placas de alabastro, grabados con largos epitafios;
plates of alabaster engraved with large epitaphs

y más de una vez, desde que empecé a leer,
and more of (than) one time from that started to read

me distraje durante la Misa o el Rosario,
me (I) distracted during the Mass or the Rosary

procurando descifrar aquellos letreros, para mí
attempting to decipher those letters for me

atravesados e ininteligibles.
crossed through and unintelligible

Una noche, camino de mi alcoba, ocurrióseme
One night (on) road of my bedroom occurred to me

hacer esta pregunta:
to make this question

- Angustias, ¿Qué hacen los muertos de la capilla,
– Angustias What do the deads of the chapel

en la noche?
in the night

Y la india, sin titubear, contestó:
And the native without hesitating answered

- Juegan al ajedrez.
— (They) play -to the- chess

Yo que casi todas las noches, al requerir la
I that almost all the nights at the going for the

bendición de mi padre, lo encontraba en la
(daily) blessing of my father him encountered in the

biblioteca jugando al ajedrez con don Pepe
library playing -to the- chess with don Pepe

Dávalos, Presidente Municipal del pueblo
Davalos President municipal of the village

comarcano, no me sorprendí de la respuesta. Un
next over not me surprised of the answer A

juego en que dos señores se sentaban frente
game in that two gentlemen themselves seated front

a frente, durante largo espacio de tiempo, sin
to front during (a) large space of time without

proferir palabra y sin mover apenas las
to utter (a) word and without to move almost the

curiosas piezas de madera que entre sí
strange pieces of wood that between themselves

tenían, y que se prestaban de manera tan
(they) had and that themselves borrowed of manner so

admirable para jugar a los soldaditos; un juego
admirable to play to the little soldiers a game

así, repito, me parecía más a propósito para
like that (I) repeat me seemed more to purpose for
appropriate

muertos que para vivos; y la contestación de
(the) dead than for (the) living and the answer of

Angustias fue convincente.
Angustias was convincing

- Sí; - continuó el ama. - Todas las noches, en
— Yes — continued the lady — All the nights in

cuanto tú te acuestas a dormir, ellos
how much you yourself lay down to sleep they

se ponen a jugar al ajedrez hasta que
themselves set to play -at the- chess until that

llega el Padre a decir misa. Entonces se
arrives the Father to say Mass Then themselves

vuelven a sus sepulcros, que son, como si
(they) return to their sepulchres that are as if

dijéramos, sus camas, y duermen durante el día.
(we) say their beds and (they) sleep during the day

Y dichas las oraciones de costumbre, por mis
And (having) said the prayers of usual for my

padres y hermanos, y otra, que para mí coleto
parents and brothers and other that for my insides

decía, por mi caballo "El Confite", quedé al
said for my horse The Sugarplum remained at the

momento dormido.
moment asleep

II

Muchos años después, cuando regresé de
Many years from then when (I) returned from

España, casado ya con mujer de mi misma
Spain married already with (a) woman of my same

estirpe, hallé las cosas en San Isidro Labrador muy
lineage found the things in Saint Isidor Farmer very

distintas de cuando me marchara. Mis padres, dos
distict from when me walked (happened) My parents two

hermanos y Angustias habían desaparecido de
brothers and Angustias had disappeared from

la vida, y don Pepe Dávalos, depuesto de su
-the- life and don Pepe Davalos deposed from his

cargo municipal, vagaba enfermo y viejo por
job municipal roamed ill and old through

los claustros, añorando las partidas de ajedrez con
the cloisters yearning for the parts (games) of chess with

"su Merced el Señor don Alonso." Noté que el
his Mercy the Lord don Alonso (I) noted that the

respetuoso cariño de muchos sirvientes había
respectful care of many servants had

amenguado, gracias a ciertos vientos de fronda
diminished thanks to certain winds of plenty

que del Norte soplaban, y sentí desde un
that from the North blew and (I) felt from a

principio marcada repulsión por el nuevo
beginning marked repulsion for the new

administrador de la Hacienda, nombrado por el
administrator of the Estate named by the

albacea de mi padre. Llamábase don Guadalupe
executor of my father (He) called himself don Guadelupe

Robles, y su aspecto insolente demostraba bien
Robles and his aspect insolent demonstrated well

a las claras que había sido antaño guerrillero
-to- the clears that (he) had been former rebel

audaz y duro cacique.
bold and hard chief

Mucho temí que la Hacienda tuviera pocos
Much (I) feared that the Estate had few

atractivos para mi mujer, pero Inés, acostumbrada
attractions for my wife but Ines accustomed

a las austeridades de su torre castellana, encontró
to the austerities of her tower Castelan found

San Isidro Labrador muy de su agrado, y
Saint Isidor Farmer much of her liking and

propuso ella misma que fijáramos allí nuestra
proposed she (her)self that (we) fix (we set up) there our

residencia.
residence

Transcurridos pocos meses, y aproximándose la
Run through (Having passed) (a) few months and approaching itself the

fiesta titular de la heredad, mi mujer, a fuer de
feast titular of the inheritance my wife at to be of

buena madrileña propuso que la fiesta fuese
good Madrid woman proposed that the feast were

celebrada con especial pompa. Preparó, pues,
celebrated with especial pomp (She) prepared then

ropas para repartir a los pobres; encargó
clothes for to divide to the poor people (she) ordered

flores para el adorno de la casa y capilla;
flowers for the decoration of the house and (the) chapel

y convidó, para que cantara Misa
and invited for that (he) sung (the) Mass

Pontifical, a cierto Prelado, a quien, desde mi
pontifical (papal, or of bishop) a certain Prelado to whom from my

infancia, llamaba yo "el tío Obispo", aunque en
infancy called I the uncle Bishop although in

realidad carecíamos de parentesco alguno.
reality (we) lacked of parenthood (relationship) any

Yo accedí gustoso, tanto por complacer a Inés,
I agreed gladly so much for to please -to- Ines

cuanto porque hallé la ocasión propicia para
as much as because (I) found the occasion appropriate for

hacer lucir gran cantidad de objetos, de los
to make shine (a) great quantity of objects of -the-

cuales, como colector entusiasta de antiguallas,
which as collector enthusiastic of antiquities
enthusiastic collector

me vanagloriaba. Al caudal no despreciable de
myself boasted At the flow not negligible of
large flow

ornamentos y vasos sagrados, que a la Hacienda
ornaments and vases sacred that at the Estate

habían donado mis antepasados, añadí yo gran
(they) had (had been) donated to my ancestors added I (a) great

acopio de objetos, hallados algunos en vetustas
gathering (heap) of objects found some in ancient

ciudades del país, traídos otros de la
cities of the country brought others from the
others brought over

Península. Era especialmente notable mi rica
peninsula Was especially notable my rich
Especially notable was

colección de plata labrada; componíase de varias
collection of silver worked composed itself of various

docenas de candeleros, grandes y pequeños,
dozens of candlesticks large and small

atriles, vasos y macetones ornamentales; no
lecterns vases and planters for decoration not

pocos blandones; algunos cálices y
(a) few large candlesticks some chalices and
{sticks for thick candles}

copones; y una custodia que me complacía yo
large cups and a monstrance that myself pleased I
I liked to

en atribuir a Juan de Arfe y Villafañe. Pero lo
in attribute to Juan of Arfe and Villafane But that

que más me agradaba y mostraba yo a mis
what most me gratified and showed I to my

amigos con el mayor orgullo, era un juego de
friends with the greatest pride was a game of
(set)

pebeteros que adquirí en Cintra. Obra de
incense vessels that (I) adquired in Cintra Work of

portugueses de pleno siglo XVIII,
(the) Portuguese of full century 18th

se comprenderá desde luego que tales
itself will understand from then that such
you will understand of course

perfumadores tenían que ser extravagantes; en
perfuming vessels had to be extravagant in

efecto, medían más de medio metro de
effect (they) measured more of half (a) meter of
(than)

altura, y afectaban la inusitada forma de
height and affected the unused form of
(put on) (unusual)

Pegasus, pero su labor era de tal forma acabada,
Pegasus but its labor was of such form finished

que en verdad podían figurar en la mejor
that in reality (they) could figure in the best

colección de objetos de arte.
collection of objects of art

Con todos esos elementos, comprendí que el
With all those elements (I) understood that the

suntuoso retablo, cuya intrincada hojarasca cubría
sumptuous altarpiece whose intricate leaf-scratch covered
(foliage pattern)

el muro frontero de la capilla con pilastras y
the wall front of the chapel with pilasters and
front wall

columnas retorcidas, frontones interrumpidos,
columns twisted frontons interrupted
(upper part of column)

ménsulas de caprichosa forma, y nichos y
supports of capricious form and niches and

doseles cobijando esculturas policromas, haría
canopies sheltering statues polychrome would make
multicolored statues

brillar el rico y si se quiere bárbaro
shine the wealth and if itself want barbarian
you want (to say it) (stupendous)

conjunto de oro y plata, como una ascua
gathering of gold and silver like an ember

refulgente; y empecé a hacer preparativos con
glowing and (I) started to make preperations with

no escaso entusiasmo.
not scarce enthusiasm
a lot of enthusiasm

Llegada la víspera de la fiesta, entré en la
Arrived the eve of the feast (I) entered in the

capilla para disponer lo necesario, y
chapel to arrange the necessary and

vínoseme a mi mente un mundo de
came-itself-to-me to my mind a world of

recuerdos. Contemplando las fúnebres alegorías, y
memories Contemplating the funeral allegories and

leyendo los letreros de las lápidas, que tanto
reading the labels of the (head)stones that so much

inquietaron mis años infantiles, vio de nuevo
disturbed my years of child (I) saw of new
child years again

mil incidentes de mi niñez y escuché,
(a) thousand incidents of my childhood and (I) heard
(occurrences)

una vez más, la voz de personas queridas, entre
one time more the voice of persons loved between

ellas Angustias, quien me aseguraba
them Angustias who me assured

dogmáticamente que mis muertos jugaban al
dogmatically that my dead ones played -to the-

ajedrez todas las noches....
chess all the nights

Dirigía yo la colocación de los distintos
Directed I the placement of the various

ornamentos, sobre el altar y presbiterio, cuando
ornaments on the altar and (the) presbytery when

acudió don Guadalupe Robles a la capilla, con
came don Guadalupe Robles to the chapel with

pretexto de consultarme no acuerdo qué
pretext of to consult me in (the) agreement that

extremo de la administración de la hacienda; y
extended from the administration of the estate and

al ver el caudal allí reunido, la codicia se
at the to see the fortune there reunited the greed itself
at seeing

reflejó en su semblante haciéndole dirigir la
reflected in his face making him direct the

mirada, mientras conversaba conmigo,
look while (he) conversed with me

de uno en otro objeto, cuya existencia ni siquiera
of one in other object which existence not surely
about one or another object

sospechaba. Entonces fue mayor mi repugnancia
(I) suspected Then was great my repugnance

por aquel hombre, y tuve desde luego tal
for that man and (I) had from then such
of course

convicción de que intentaría robarme, que durante
conviction of that (he) intended to rob me that during

toda la noche no pude despedir este
all the night not (I) could dismiss this

pensamiento de mi mente, y abandoné el
thought from my mind and (I) abandoned the

lecho muy temprano, cuando aún dormían en
bed very early when still slept in

silencio amos y sirvientes.
silence masters and servants

Con la primera claridad del amanecer, penetré
With the first clarity of the dawning (I) entered

en la capilla. A primera vista, la mayor parte de
in the chapel At first view the largest part of

los objetos permanecían en los sitios en que la
the objects (had) remained in the sites in that the

víspera se colocaran, pero ¡júzguese
eve themselves (they) were placed but judge yourself

cuál sería mi asombro, al ver que gran
how would be my surprise at the to see that (a) large
at seeing

número de candeleros, jarrones y demás yacían
number of candlesticks vases and more laid

diseminados por el suelo en el más completo
spread out on the floor in the most complete

desorden! Sólo quedaban en pie, arrinconados en
disorder Only remained in foot cornered in

un ángulo debajo del coro, cuatro objetos. Me
a angle under of the choir four objects Myself
(corner)

aproximé, y un escalofrío recorrió todo mi
(I) approached and a shiver ran over all my

cuerpo. ¡Los muertos habían jugado una partida de
body The dead had played a part (game) of

ajedrez! Sí, allí en el rincón, sobre la loseta
chess Yes there in the corner on the tile

blanca, estaba un blandón, y enfrente de él,
white was a thick candlestick and in front of him (it)

salvada una hilera de cuadros, y ocupando sus
saved (separated by) a row of squares and occupying their

respectivas casillas, un jarrón, un candelero
respective squares a vase a candlestick

pequeño y uno de los perfumadores, éste el más
small and one of the perfume vessels this the most

próximo al muro. Sí, esas tres piezas - el
close to the wall Yes those three pieces the

alfil, el peón y el caballo, - habían dado jaque
bishop the pawn and the horse (knight) had given chess

mate al blandón o sea, al Rey!
mate to the thick candlestick or be it to the King

Después de algún tiempo, pude dominarme, y
After -of- some time (I) could dominate myself and
(control myself)

con mano trémula repuse en sus sitios los
with (a) hand trempling (I) reset in their sites the
(I put back)

diferentes objetos, para que nadie, más que yo,
different objects for that no one most that I
(so) especially me

se diera cuenta del suceso.
himself gave count of the happened
would notice what happened

La fiesta fue celebrada debidamente, y tanto el
The feast was celebrated duly and so much the

Obispo como los amigos que acudieron a nuestra
Bishop as the friends that arrived at our

invitación, se hicieron lenguas de la
invitation themselves made tongues of the
praised

hermosura y riqueza de mi colección. Pero yo
beauty and richness of my collection But I
(wealth)

prestaba escasa atención a tales elogios,
loaned hardly attention to such compliments
(gave)

embargada mi mente con el enigma y las
loaded my mind with the mystery and the

sospechas que abrigaba contra don Guadalupe
suspicions that (I) harbored against don Guadalupe

Robles. Estas aumentaron, cuando lo sorprendí,
Robles These increased when him (I) surprised

al atardecer, en la penumbra del corredor,
at the dawning in the semi-darkness of the corridor

hablando en voz baja con Joaquín, su
talking in voice low with Joaquin his

mozo de estribo y hombre de toda confianza.
boy of stirrup and man of total trust
groom

Simulé no haberlos visto, y pasé de largo;
(I) pretended not to have them seen and passed of length
passed by

pero resolví empaquetar mis antiguallas y
but (I) resolved pack up my antiques and

remitirlas a México, cuanto antes, mientras
sent them back to Mexico how much before while

encontraba yo la oportunidad de deshacerme del
found I the opportunity of to rid myself of the

Administrador.
administrator

No sé cuanto tiempo después de haber
Not (I) know how much time after of to have

logrado conciliar el sueño, rasgó el silencio de
managed to reconcile (to find) the sleep tore the silence of

aquella noche tal grito de terror, que sigue
that night such (a) scream of terror that continues

y seguirá retumbando en mis oídos, mientras
and will continue to reverberate in my ears while

yo viva. Lo oyó mi mujer y despertó asustada;
I live It heard my wife and (she) woke up in fright

lo oyeron los sirvientes todos, y en breves
it heard the servants all and in short

momentos, los claustros fueron poblándose
moments the cloisters were populating themselves

de sombras, que inquirían con voces de miedo
of (with) shadows that inquiered with voices of fear

qué acontecía.
what (had) happened

Tomé una linterna, y seguido por los más
(I) took a lantern and followed by the most

resueltos, dirigí mis medrosos pasos hacia el
resolved (I) directed my fearful steps towards the

sitio de donde el grito pareciera proceder. La
site from where the scream (had) seemed to proceed (to emanate) The

puerta de la sacristía estaba abierta y
door of the sacristy was open and

comprendí que mis sospechas se habían
(I) understood that my suspicions themselves had

confirmado. Entramos. Ni en la sacristía, ni en
confirmed (We) entered Neither in the sacristy nor in

la capilla, había más luz que la escasa claridad
the chapel had (there was) more light than the scarce clarity (light)

que penetraba por cúpulas y ventanas, y
that penetrated through (the) cupolas and windows and

al principio nada pudimos distinguir; pero, a
at the beginning nothing (we) could distinguish but by

poco, la trémula luz de la linterna nos hizo ver
little the wavering light of the lantern us made see

que todos los objetos de plata, absolutamente
that all the objects of silver absolutely

todos, se hallaban amontonados bajo el
all themselves found in a heap under the

coro, cercando, aprisionando en el rincón, a don
choir encircling imprisoned in the corner -to- don

Guadalupe Robles, quien, con el cuerpo echado
Guadalupe Robles who with the body thrown

para atrás, como reculando, extendía ambos
to (the) back as (if) recoiling extended both

brazos contra los muros de aquel ángulo de la
arms against the walls of that corner of the

capilla. Tenía los ojos fuera de sus órbitas, y
chapel (He) had the eyes outside of its orbits and

todo su semblante era imagen del terror. Lo
all his face was image of the terror Him

llamé por su nombre, me miró fijamente y
(I) called by his name me (he) watched fixedly and

fue su única contestación una carcajada...
was his only answer a loud laugh

El Papagayo De Huichilobos

EL PAPAGAYO DE HUICHILOBOS
The Parrot Of Huichilobos

Cuando el Duque de Ayamonte me nombró
When the duke of Ayamonte me named

bibliotecario y archivero de su ilustre casa,
librarian and archivist of his illustrious house

creí que mi vida iba a deslizarse
(I) believed that my life went to slide itself (glide by)

tranquilamente en los bajos de su palacio de
calmly in the lows (basement) of his palace of

Madrid; y hasta vio en lontananza la
Madrid and up to that (I) saw in (the) distance the

publicación de varios trabajos de índole histórica,
publication of various works of character history

que desde hacía muchos años codiciaba, y los
that from (it) had many years (I) longed after and the
(I tried to make)

cuales, sin embargo, permanecen inéditos, su
which without hinder remained unpublished their
(doubt)

mayor parte todavía dentro de mi tintero. Todo lo
major part still inside of my ink bottle All the

contrario de lo que yo esperaba, el magnate
contrary of that what I expected the magnate
(powerful man)

resultó ser un investigador incansable, y
resulted to be an investigator tireless and
(turned out)

mientras él dedicaba largas horas a explorar en
while he dedicated long hours to explore in

los archivos de la Corte, me enviaba a menudo
the archives of the Court me (he) sent -at- often

en busca de documentos a Provincias.
in search of documents at (the) Provinces
(in)

Así fue como en el verano pasado da con
Thus (it) was how in the summer passed (I) gave with
last summer (I arrived)

mis cansados huesos en la histórica y hoy
my tired bones in the historical and today

muerta ciudad de Alcalá del Río, en lugar de
dead city of Alcala of the River in place of

marcharme, como hubiera deseado, a
the march myself as (I) had wanted to

veranear a la costa. Estaba yo en vísperas
spend the summer on the coast Was I on eves
(the eve)

de contraer matrimonio, y aunque el sueldo
of (to) contract marriage and although the salary

que disfrutaba no era corto, no desperdiciaba
that (I) enjoyed not was short not (I) wasted
(small)

medio alguno de hacer economías. Por lo tanto,
means any of to make economies For that much
any means (budget)

no quise alojarme en el principal hotel de
not (I) wanted to stay over myself in the main hotel of

la localidad, que a pesar de ser malo era caro,
the locality that at weight of to be small was expensive
in spite

sino que busqué más modesta vivienda.
but -that- (I) searched (a) more modest dwelling

Después de recorrer varias fondas, decidí aceptar
After of to roam various inns (I) decided to accept

la habitación que en su casa me brindaba
the living quarters that in her house me offered

cierta viuda, mediante muy reducido estipendio.
(a) certain widow by means of (because of) (a) very reduced stipend (rent)

Era una pieza humildísima, sin duda alguna,
(It) was a piece (room) humble without doubt any

pero limpia como una patena, y lo que más
but clean as a paten (silver plate) and that what more

me atrajo fue el risueño aspecto de su balcón.
me attracted was the smiling (happy) aspect of her balcony

Como soy ignorante en botánica, no podré
As (I) am ignorant in botanics not (I) will be able

decir con exactitud qué plantas eran las que tan
to say with accuracy what plants were those that so

profusamente lo adornaban, pero me parece que
profusely it adorned but me (it) seems that

las que crecían en el viejo bote de petróleo
those that grew in the old pot of petroleum

eran azáleas, y estoy seguro de que había
were azaleas and (I) am sure of that (it) had (there were)

hortensias en una barrica, geranios en varios
hydrangeas in a cask geraniums in various

cacharros desportillados, y "no-me-olvides" en
crockery chipped and forget-me-not's in

una lata de sardinas. Desde el interior del
a can of sardines From the interior of the

cuarto, sólo se veía el muro de la torre de la
quarter(s) (room) only itself saw the wall of the tower of the

Catedral, pues la calle que mediaba era
cathedral since the street that (it) came out to was

sumamente estrecha; pero cuando me asomé
extremely narrow but when myself (I) went out

al balcón, grata fue mi sorpresa al hallar
to the balcony pleasant was my surprise at the find
to find

que había delante del famoso templo una
that (it) had in front of the famous temple a
(there was) (church)

plazoleta con árboles, y que como aquella era
small square with trees and that as that was

la parte más alta de la ciudad, dominaba la vista
the part most high of the city dominated the view

las extensas y pintorescas vegas del contorno.
the extensive and pictoresque meadows of the contour
(surroundings)

Nunca he dormido tan bien como la primera
Never (I) have slept so well as the first

noche que pasé en aquella modesta alcoba.
night that (I) passed in that modest alcove
(bedroom)

A pesar de haber dejado abierta la ventana, pues
At weight of to have left open the window since
In spite

lo permitía la temperatura, no sufrí ruido
it permitted the temperature not (I) suffered noise

molesto de ninguna especie. Al contrario,
hindering of any sort At the contrary

creo que me arrulló suavemente el constante
(I) believe that me cooed gently the constant

y sonoro toque de campanas.
and sonorous strike of (the) bells

Desperté temprano, como es mi costumbre, y
(I) woke up early as is my habit and

desde el lecho empecé a admirar de nuevo el
from the bed started to admire of new the
again

grato aspecto de mi balcón florido: las
pleasurable aspect of my balcony flowered the

hortensias, con sus esferas de azul y rosa; las
hydrangeas with their spheres of blue and pink the

azáleas y geranios, con sus variados tonos de
azaleas and geraniums with their various shades of

rojo y blanco; mas ¿qué era esa flor maravillosa,
red and white but what was that flower wondrous

en el centro de todas, en la cual
in the center of all -in- -the- which

no había yo reparado la víspera?
not had I noticed the eve
I had not noticed (last night)

Salté del lecho, y vio con sorpresa que no
(I) jumped from the bed and saw with surprise that not

era flor alguna, sino un pájaro que se posaba
(it) was flower any but a bird that itself posed

en el barandal del balcón. Me acerqué con
on the railing of the balcony Myself approached with
I approached

grandísima cautela, por miedo de ahuyentarlo. Al
(the) greatest care for fear of to make it flee At the

principio lo tomé por un loro, pero enseguida
beginning it (I) took for a parakeet but then

comprendí que era de mayor tamaño. No
(I) understood that (it) was of larger size Not

intentaré describir su maravilloso plumaje, porque
(I) will try to describe its wonderful plumage because

no podría hacerlo. Sólo diré que me hizo
not (I) could do that Only (I) will say that (on) me (it) made

la impresión de una joya inmensa, esmaltada con
the impression of a jewel huge enameled with

los colores más vivos que puedan imaginarse:
the colors most lively that can to imagine themselves (be imagined)

verde, azul, rojo, amarillo....
green blue red yellow

No sé cuánto tiempo permanecí asombrado.
Not (I) know how much time (I) remained surprised

Sólo sé que repentinamente experimenté una
Only (I) know that suddenly (I) experienced a

sensación extraña, una codicia exagerada de
sensation strange a longing exagerated of

poseer tan exótica ave. Sentí lo que debe
to possess such (an) exotic bird (I) felt that what must

sentir el ladrón cuando se propone
feel the thief when himself proposes

apoderarse de lo ajeno, y me da plena
to empower himself (to seize) of that of others and me (I) gave full

cuenta, en aquellos instantes, de que cometería
account in those instances of that (I) would commit

cualquier crimen, con tal de hacerme con ese
any crime with such of to make me (to get myself) with that

pájaro de rico plumaje. Largo espacio de tiempo
parrot of rich plumage (A) Long space of time

permanecí inmóvil, pensando en la mejor manera
(I) remained immobile thinking on (of) the best way

de llevar a cabo mi intento. El ave movía
of to take to end my intent The bird moved

ligeramente las alas, que brillaban fantásticamente
lightly the wings that shone fantastically

como abanicos de esmeraldas; y con la certeza
like fans of emeralds and with the certainty

de que no podría yo asirla viva, decidí darle
of that not could I grab it alive (I) decided to give it

muerte. Con la mayor cautela, tomé un grueso
death With the most care (I) took a thick

bastón que solía acompañarme en mis viajes, y
stick that used to accompany me in my travels and

conteniendo la respiración y avanzando unos
containing the breath and advancing some

pasos, le asesté tremendo golpe sobre el ala
steps it (I) dealt (a) tremendous blow on the wing

izquierda, que sonó seco y lastimero contra el
left that sounded dry and plaintive against the

barandal de hierro. Cayó el pájaro a la calle y
railing of iron Fell the bird to the street and

yo, por lo pronto, no me atreví a asomarme,
I for the moment not myself dared to go out myself

temiendo que algún transeúnte fuese testigo de mi
fearing that some passerby was witness of my

acción nefanda. Un escalofrío recorrió mi cuerpo;
action nefarious A shiver ran across my body

me sentí culpable y avergonzado, como debió
myself (I) felt guilty and ashamed as had to

sentirse el viejo marinero del poema cuando
feel himself the old mariner from the poem when

dio muerte al albatros con su ballesta.
(he) gave death to the albatros with his crossbow

Por fin me asomé. Ni el pájaro yacía en la
By end myself (I) got out Neither the bird lay on the
At last

casi desierta calle ni advertí trazas de sangre
almost deserted street nor (I) noticed traces of blood

en el barandal de la ventana. A poco tuve todo
in the railing of the window At little (I) had all

aquello por una alucinación y quedé
that for a hallucination and (I) remained

desconcertado. ¿Sería un preludio de locura?
disconcerted Would (it) be a prelude to madness

--

No pude encontrar en el Archivo de Protocolos
Not (I) could encounter (find) in the archive of protocols

de Alcalá del Río los documentos que el Duque
of Alcala of the River the documents that the Duke

de Ayamonte necesitaba, y el encargado de
of Ayamonte needed and the person in charge of

aquella oficina me indicó que quizá obrarían
that office to me indicated that maybe (they) would be

en el de la Catedral. Provisto de una carta de
in that of the Cathedral Provided of (with) a card of

presentación para el Deán, me encaminé
presentation for the Dean myself (I) set on the road

al famoso edificio, y desde el momento que
to the famous edifice (building) and from the moment that

penetré en él, olvidé por completo la misión
(I) penetrated in it (I) forgot for complete completely the mission

que me llevaba allí. Del Presbiterio al Coro,
that me took there From the Presbytery to the Choir

y de capilla en capilla, fui recorriendo el
and from chapel in chapel (I) was walking around the

templo y admirando las múltiples bellezas que
temple (church) and admiring the multiple beauties that

encierra. Como acontece siempre en los recintos
(it) encloses Like happens always in the enclosures

históricos, varios guías se ofrecieron a
historical various guides themselves offered to

acompañarme, pero yo los rechacé a todos,
accompany me but I -them- refused to all

deseando saborear a solas tanta obra de arte.
desiring to taste -at- singles (alone) so much work of art

Repentinamente oí una exclamación de
Suddenly (I) heard an exclamation of

sorpresa y, volviendo el rostro, me encontré
surprise and turning the face myself encountered (found)

cara a cara con el Padre Montero, mi antiguo
face to face with the Father Montero my old

condiscípulo, a quien no había visto en cinco
fellow disciple (fellow student) -to- whom not (I) had seen in five

años. Fungía de Sacristán mayor de la
years (He) functioned of Sachristan mayor of the

Catedral y llevaba un manojo de enormes llaves,
Cathedral and carried a bunch of enormous keys

pues era hora de cerrar el templo, para volver
since (it) was hour of to close the church for to return

a abrirlo a las tres de la tarde. Inútil me
to open it at the three of the afternoon Needless to me

parece relatar el gusto que me dio volver a
(it) seems to tell the pleasure that me (it) gave to return to

ver a tan buen amigo mío. Convidóme a
see -to- such good friend (of) mine (He) Invited me to

almorzar y prometió enseñarme él mismo,
have breakfast and (he) promised to teach me he himself

después, las mil maravillas que poseía aquel
after the thousand wonders that possessed that

cabildo	y	que	raras	veces	se	exponían
church chapter	and	that	seldom	times	themselves	were shown

al	público.
to the	public

Sonaban	las	tres,	cuando	el	Padre	Montero	y	yo,
Sounded	the	three	when	the	Father	Montero	and	I
It struck three o'clock								

empezamos	a	recorrer	el	salón	de	cabildos,	las
started	to	walk around	the	salon	of	churchmen	the

sacristías	mayor	y	menor,	la	clavería,	el
sacristy	large	and	minor	the	key room	the

camarín	de	Nuestra	Señora	de	las	Rosas,	el
dressing room	of	Our	Lady	of	the	Roses	the

vestuario	y	demás	dependencias.	Sólo	con
locker room	and	more	annexes	Only	with

enumerar	las	múltiples	bellezas	que	me
to enumerate	the	multiple	beautiful things	that	me

mostró	se	llenaría	un	volumen;	y	cuando
(he) showed	himself	filled	a	volume (book)	and	when

creí que había terminado mi visita, me
(I) believed that (I) had ended my visit me

anunció con cierta satisfacción:
(he) announced with certain satisfaction

- Te falta ver lo principal: el tesoro.
You lack (need) to see the main (thing) the treasury

Ante una puerta de roble con remaches de hierro,
Before a gate of oak with rivets of iron

que al principio creí daría acceso a la
that at the beginning (I) believed would give access to the

escalera de la torre, un canónigo nos esperaba
stairs of the tower a canon {ecclesiastic} us awaited

rezando su oficio. Hechas las presentaciones
praying his canon prayer Made the introductions

del caso, el Tesorero abrió la pesada puerta de
of the case the Treasurer opened the heavy gate of

madera, y apareció otra, moderna,
wood and (there) appeared (an)other modern

semejante a la de una caja fuerte. La abrió a
similar at that of a box strong It (he) opened at
safe

su vez, y en seguida una fuerte reja, que todavía
its turn and in following a strong bar that still

impedía el paso. Pero ni ese aparato de
impeded the pass(ing) But neither that apparatus of

seguridad haría sospechar la riqueza que en
security would make suspect the richness that in
(wealth)

aquel aposento se guardaba. Más de una hora
that chamber itself (was) guarded More of an hour
(than)

permanecimos admirando custodias, cálices, atriles,
(we) remained admiring monstrances chalices lecterns

estatuas y toda clase de joyas, cuyo interés
statues and all class of jewels whose interest

acrecentaban los eruditos informes del canónigo.
were increased by the erudite informations of the canonical

Súbitamente, dejé escapar un grito de sorpresa.
Suddenly (I) let escape a shout of surprise

¡Allí, delante de mis ojos, encerrado dentro de
There before -of- my eyes enclosed inside of

una vitrina y posado dentro de una peaña de
a glass case and set inside of a pedestal of

oro, se hallaba un pájaro idéntico a mi
gold itself (was) located a bird identical to my

visitante de aquella mañana! Estaba cuajado de
visitor of that morning (It) was curdled of

esmeraldas, rubíes, diamantes, en fin, de la más
emeralds rubies diamonds in end (all) of the most

rica pedrería que pueda imaginarse; y labrado
rich gemstones that (one) can imagine oneself and worked

todo con tal arte, que a primera vista parecía
all with such art that at first sight (it) seemed

estar vivo.
to be alive

- Comprendo su emoción, - dijo el canónigo. -
(I) understand your emotion said the canon {ecclesiastic}

Está reputada esta joya como una de las más
(It) is famous this jewel like one of the most

notables de que hay noticia. Con decir a usted
notable of that has notice With to say to you
(there is) (known)

que el Museo Británico ha ofrecido millones, así
that the Museum British has offered millions so

como suena, millones, por ella, se dará
as (it) sounds millions for her yourself will give

usted cuenta de su alto mérito artístico y valor
you count of its high merit artistic and worth

intrínseco. Pero el Cabildo antes enajenaría
intrinsic But the church chapter before (it) would sell
would rather sell

todo lo que hemos visto que deshacerse de esta
all it that (we) had seen than dispose herself of this

incomparable joya. Fue en un tiempo el adorno
incomparable jewel (It) was in one time the ornament

principal del templo mayor de los aztecas; uno
main of the temply major of the Aztecs one

de los conquistadores de México lo arrancó del
of the conquerors of Mexico it grabbed from the

altar mismo del famoso "Huichilobos", y lo
altar same of the famous Huichilobos and it

trajo a Carlos V, quien lo donó a esta
brought to Carlos (the) 5th who it donated to this

Santa Iglesia.
Saintly Church

Viendo que permanecía yo estupefacto, quiso
Seeing that remained I stupefied (he) felt like

que mi admiración fuese mayor, y abrió la
that my admiration was great and opened the

vitrina para que examinara a mis anchas aquel
showcase for to examine at my shoulders that

portento de orfebrería. Tomó la joya en sus
wonder of goldsmithing (He) took the jewel in his

manos, y al acercarla a la luz, para mejor
hands and at the approaching her to the light for better

mostrármela, exhaló una exclamación de espanto.
to show her exhaled an exclamation of terror

- ¡Dios me valga! ¿Qué es esto?
God me avails What is this

¡El papagayo estaba lastimosamente maltratado en
The parrot was pitifully maltreated (damaged) in

el ala izquierda, como si hubiese sido golpeado
the wing left like if (it) had been struck

con un martillo! Imagínese la consternación
with a hammer Imagine yourself the consternation

del canónigo y del sacristán mayor. En
of the canon and of the sacristy mayor In

cuanto a mí, sentí como si fuera el autor de
how much to me (I) felt like if (I) was the author of

aquel atentado y temí que lo revelara mi
that attack and feared that it (I) revealed my

semblante. Pero mis compañeros estaban
countenance But my companions were

demasiado ocupados en examinar el desperfecto,
too occupied in to examine the imperfectness

para fijarse en mi persona.
for to focus themselves on my person

- ¿Cómo ha podido ser esto? ¿Quién pudo llegar
How has been able to be this Who could arrive

hasta aquí y cometer tan audaz sacrilegio? -
up to here and commit such bold sacrilige

Exclamaban ambos escandalizado.
Exclaimed both scandalized

El Tesorero ordenó al Padre Montero que
The Treasurer ordered -to- the Father Montero that

avisase al Deán, y la nueva corrió
(he) advise -to- the Dean and the news ran (spread)

rápidamente, pues a los pocos momentos
rapidly since at the few moments

acudieron varios canónigos y prebendados,
arrived various canons and prebendaries {honorary canon}

quienes anunciaron que Su Eminencia en persona
who anounced that His Eminence in person

iría a comprobar con sus propios ojos el
would go to ascertain with his own eyes the

inexplicable y audaz atentado.
unexplainable and bold attack

--

Mientras se daban los pasos oportunos
While themselves gave the steps opportune
(went through) (necessary)

para descubrir al autor del delito, dispuso el
for to discover -to- the author of the crime arranged the

Cardenal Arzobispo de Alcalá del Río que la
Cardinal Achbishop of Alcala of the River that the

maltratada joya fuera guardada dentro de un cofre
maltreated jewel was guarded inside of a box
(damaged)

fuerte que había en el Tesoro, y que hasta
strong that had in the Treasury and that until
(there was)

nueva orden se suspendiesen las visitas del
new order themselves (they) suspended the visits of the
were suspended

público.
public

Oprimido por la vergüenza y el temor, me
Oppressed by the shame and the fear myself

despedí del Padre Montero, y olvidando
(I) dismissed from the Father Montero and forgetting

por completo la búsqueda de documentos que a
for complete the search of documents that to
completely

la Catedral me había llevado, dirigí mis pasos
the Cathedral me had brought (I) directed my steps

lentamente hacia mi alojamiento.
slowly towards my accomodation

Renuncio a describir mi estado de ánimo durante
(I) renounce to describe my state of spirit during
(I don't want) (mind)

el resto de aquel día. Quise rechazar mi
the rest of that day (I) wanted to repel my

constante preocupación por medio de la lectura,
constant preoccupation by means of the reading

pero dio la casualidad de que la única obra que
but gave the chance coincidentally of that the only work that

había llevado conmigo era la Historia de Bernal
(I) had taken with me was the History of Bernal

Díaz del Castillo, y ella, lejos de
Diaz of the Castle and she (that) far from

proporcionarme distracción, daba rienda suelta a
proportion me (lend me) distraction gave rein loose free rein to

los más extraños pensamientos. Dejé el libro y
the most strange thoughts (I) left the book and

salí a pasear por las vegas, hasta el
went out to walk through the meadows until the

anochecer. Cuando regresé a mi alcoba me
falling of the night When (I) returned to my bedroom me

sentí calenturiento y me metí entre sábanas;
(I) felt fevered and myself (I) put between sheets

pero	sólo	logré	conciliar	intranquilo	y
but	only	(I) managed	to reconcile	(a) restless	and

mil	veces	interrumpido	sueño.	Recuerdo	que
(a) thousand	times	interrupted	sleep	(I) remember	that

aquella	noche	fui	testigo	de	los	episodios	más
that	night	(I) was	witness	of	the	episodes	most

sangrientos	de	la	conquista	de	México.	Los
bloody	of	the	conquest	of	Mexico	The

sacerdotes	aztecas	abrían	el	pecho	de	sus
priests	aztec	opened	the	breast	of	their

víctimas	y	arrancábanles	el	corazón,	palpitante
victims	and	ripped from them	the	heart	beating

aún,	para	ofrecerlo	al	terrible	Huichilobos,	que
still	for	to offer it	to the	terrible	Huichilobos	that

presidía	el	Cu	mayor...	Constantemente	se	oía
presided	the	Cu {Aztec culture}	mayor	Constantly	oneself	heard

el	rumor	de	la	pelea	y	arroyos	de	sangre	por
the	sound	of	the	battle	and	streams	of	blood	by

todos lados me cercaban... Retumbó en mis oídos
all sides me neared Rumbled in my ears

el "triste sonido" del tambor que, según Bernal
the sad sound of the drum that according Bernal

Díaz, podía oírse a dos leguas de distancia, y
Diaz could hear itself (be heard) at two leagues of distance and

desperté excitado. La Campana mayor de la
(I) awoke excited The bell large of the

Catedral sonaba lúgubremente.
Cathedral sounded (struck) lugubriously

--

Con la codiciada aurora, recobré la tranquilidad
With the coveted dawn (I) recovered the tranquility

de espíritu. Trabajé todo el día en el archivo
of spirit (I) worked all the day in the archive

del Cabildo, en donde pude hallar los
of the church chapter -in- where (I) could find the

documentos que buscaba, y hasta llegué a
documents that (I) searched and up to arrived to
(managed)

olvidar los extraños sucesos de la víspera.
forget the strange happenings of the eve
(evening before)

Pero al llegar a mi habitación en la tarde,
But at the to arrive at my room in the afternoon
when I arrived

encontré que me aguardaba allí el Padre
(I) found that me awaited there the Father

Montero. Al verlo me sentí de nuevo
Montero At the to see him -myself- (I) felt of new
At seeing him again

avergonzado y culpable.
ashamed and guilty

- ¡Hola! - Dije, procurando demostrar completa
Hello (I) said trying to demonstrate complete

tranquilidad. - ¡Cuánto gusto de verte! ¿Quieres
calm How much joy of to see you (You) like

que demos un paseo por las márgenes del río,
that (we) give a walk by the margins of the river

antes de que llegue la noche?
before of that arrives the night

- Rafael, - exclamó, sin hacer caso de mi
Rafael (he) exclaimed without to make case of my

pregunta. - ¿Te acuerdas del papagayo de
question You remember (of) the parrot of

Huichilobos que viste ayer?
Huichilobos that (you) saw yesterday

- Sí, - dije casi como un reto. -
Yes (I) said almost like a convict

¿Se descubrió ya el autor del atentado?
Itself discovered already the author of the attack
Was discovered

- Eso no sería fácil en tan corto espacio de
That not would be easy in such short space of

tiempo. Lo que quiero contarte, puesto que
time That what (I) want to tell you put that
in so much that

confío en tu discreción, es lo siguiente: Has
(I) confide in your discretion is the following (You) have

de saber que Su Eminencia, que es hombre
of to know that His Eminence that (who) is man

activo, envió ayer mismo un mensaje a la
active sent yesterday same a message to the

Corte, para que viniese en seguida uno de los
Court for that comes in followed then one of the

mejores joyeros y restaurase cuanto antes el
best jewelers and repairs how much before the

desperfecto causado al papagayo. Llegó en
imperfection caused to the parrot (He) arrived in

el tren del medio día y el Deán, el Tesorero
the train of the half day and the Dean the Treasurer

y yo hemos ido esta tarde a recoger la joya
and I have gone this afternoon to get the jewel

para entregársela; pero, calcula ¡cuál sería
for to hand over it but count how would be

nuestra sorpresa, al abrir el cofre y ver
our surprise at the to open at opening the box and to see

que el papagayo ha desaparecido! Cómo ha
that the parrot has disappeared How has

podido llegar hasta allí el ladrón, nadie ha
been able to arrive until there the thief nobody has

podido explicárselo.
been able to explain it

Instintivamente nos habíamos acercado a la
Instinctively us (we) had approached to the

ventana, pues la puesta de sol prometía ser
window since the setting of (the) sun promised to be

hermosísima aquella tarde. Las gárgolas y demás
very beautiful that evening The gargoyles and other

partes salientes de la enorme catedral tenían
parts sticking out from the enormous cathedral had

ya perfiles de fuego, y las copas de los
already profiles (silhouettes) of fire and the cups (crowns) of the

árboles de la plazoleta y hasta las hortensias de
trees of the little square and up to (even) the hortensias of

mi balcón empezaban a teñirse de carmín.
my balcony started to dye themselves of (with) carmine

Súbitamente, mi compañero dio un grito de
Suddenly my companion gave (uttered) a shout of

sorpresa. Dirigiendo la mirada hacia el lugar que
surprise Directing the look towards the place that

febrilmente señalaba, vio al Papagayo de
feverishly (he) signaled (I) saw the Parrot of

Huichilobos, a poca distancia de nosotros, posado
Huichilobos at little distance from us perched

sobre un saliente de la torre.
on a protruding (ledge) of the tower

- ¡Es idéntico! - exclamó.
(It) is identical (he) exclaimed

- No, - dije con bastante calma. - Es el
No (I) said with enough calm (It) is the

mismo. Está vivo, pero tiene rota el ala
same (It) is alive but has broken the wing

izquierda. Yo mismo se la he roto.
left I myself itself it have broken

El Padre Montero me miró con extrañeza
The Father Montero me watched with strangeness
(a strange expression)

y vio que sus trémulos labios iban a formular
and (I) was that his trembling lips went to form

una pregunta; pero en ese momento el ave movió
a question but in that moment the bird moved

las alas, que brillaron a la luz del ocaso, como
the wings that shone at the light of the sunset as
(in)

si cayera una cascada de gemas dentro de una
if fell a waterfall of gems inside of a

hoguera, y tendió el vuelo en dirección
bonfire and (he) set out the flight in direction

nuestra. Vino a posarse de nuevo sobre el
our (He) came to set himself of new on the
again

barandal del balcón. ¡Sí, estaba allí el Papagayo
railing of the balcony Yes was there the Parrot

de Huichilobos, al alcance de nuestras manos,
of Huichilobos at the reach of our hands

y no osábamos tocarlo! Contuvimos la
and not (we) dared to touch it (We) contained the

respiración y no nos movimos durante largo
breathing and not us moved during (a) long

espacio de tiempo, fascinados por el inesperado
space of time fascinated by the unexpected

suceso.
happening

Con no sé qué supremo esfuerzo de la
With not (I) know what supreme effort of the

voluntad, el Padre Montero súbitamente procuró
will the Father Montero suddenly attempted

apresarlo. Pero el ave se le escapó de entre
to catch it But the bird itself him escaped from between

las manos, y tendió el vuelo hacia el Occidente.
the hands and set out the flight to the West

Yo quedé extasiado, viendo al pájaro
I remained in rapture seeing -to- the bird

alejarse por los aires, lenta y
move away itself through the air slow and

majestuosamente, hasta convertirse en minúsculo
majestically until to convert itself in (a) miniscule

punto de luz, hasta perderse en lontananza como
point of light until to loose itself in (the) distance as

si se hundiera con el sol en el horizonte.
if itself sunk with the sun on the horizon

Al volver el rostro, advertí que el Padre
At the turn the face (I) noticed that the Father

Montero permanecía inmóvil con la mirada fija en
Montero remained immobile with the look fixed on

la abierta palma de su mano. En ella brillaban
the open palm of his hand In her (it) shone

cuatro esmeraldas y tres rubíes de gran tamaño.
four emeralds and three rubies of great weight

El Amo Viejo
El Amo Viejo

EL AMO VIEJO
The Master Old
The Old Master

La familia Hernández de Sandoval, opulenta hace
The family Hernandez of Sandoval opulent until

diez años y hoy casi en la miseria, era una
ten years (ago) and today almost in the misery was one
(poverty)

de las más respetables de la ciudad de México.
of the most respectable of the city of Mexico

Como base principal de su fortuna figuraban las
As basis main of their fortune figured the
main basis

extensas haciendas que poseía, desde los
extensive estates that (it) possessed since the

tiempos de la conquista, en el hoy denominado
times of the conquering in the today called

Estado de Morelos, comarca fertilísima, en donde
state of Morelos region very fertile in which

se cultiva con preferencia la caña de azúcar.
oneself cultivates with preference the cane of sugar

Conservan muchas de las haciendas mexicanas el
Keep many of the estates mexican the

carácter de fortalezas que supieron darles sus
character of fortress that knew (managed) to give them their

primeros poseedores, mientras que otras, que no
first owners while that others that not

se distinguen por su arquitectura, abundan,
themselves distinguish for their architecture abound

en cambio, en bellezas naturales; todo lo cual
in change (the opposite) in beautiful natural (natural beauties) all that which

hace que una visita a una de estas fincas no
makes that a visit to one of those estates not

carezca, generalmente, de interés.
lacks generally of interest

A pesar de la estrecha amistad que unía a los
At weight of the tight friendship that united to the
In spite of

Hernández de Sandoval con mi familia, desde
Hernandez of Sandoval with my family since

largos años, no había yo tenido ocasión de visitar
long years not had I had occasion of to visit

ninguna de sus haciendas, aunque ellos sí
none of their estates although they yes
(any) (indeed)

habían pasado largas temporadas en la nuestra,
had passed long stays in the ours

situada en el centro del país; de manera que,
situated in the center of the country of manner that
so that

en cuanto se ofreció la oportunidad de
in how much itself offered the opportunity of

acompañar al hijo de la casa, Antonio,
to accompany to the son of the house Antonio

pudiendo desprenderme de mis no múltiples, pero
being able to detach myself from my not many but

sí imprescindibles quehaceres, la aproveché
indeed essential what-to-do's (tasks) it (I) approved

gustoso para ir en tan grata compañía a
with pleasure for to go in such pleasant company to

recorrer la finca principal de su casa, célebre por
tour the estate main of his house famous for

su riqueza y encantos naturales.
its richness and enchantments natural

Salimos de México en la noche de un diez de
(We) left from Mexico in the night of about ten eleven of

agosto, y llegamos en la madrugada a la
August and arrived in the morning at the

histórica ciudad de la Puebla de los Angeles. Todo
historical city of the village of the Angels All

el día siguiente lo pasamos a bordo del
the day following it (we) passed on board of the

ferrocarril, viaje molesto por el excesivo calor
train journey molested (bothered) by the excessive heat

que se dejaba sentir y que nos quitó toda
that itself let feel and that us removed all

gana de admirar el trayecto, rico y variado en
lust of to admire the way rich and varied in

cultivos y panorama.
crops and views

Cansados y agobiados por la alta temperatura,
Tired and overwhelmed by the high termperature

llegamos a las primeras horas de la noche a una
(we) arrived at the first hours of the night at a

pequeña estación, de cuyo nombre indígena no
small station of whose name indigenous not

quiero acordarme, y en donde nos esperaba
(I) want to remember myself and in where us awaited

el Administrador de la hacienda y varios mozos,
the administrator of the estate and various boys

con sendas caballerías. Emprendimos desde luego
with two horses (We) undertook from after
after that

la caminata, y, ya fuera porque la noche en
the walk (road) and already outside because the night in

el campo se hallaba relativamente fresca,
the field itself found was relatively cool

comparada con las molestias del ferrocarril, o
compared with the abuses of the train or

porque veía yo próximo el fin de la jornada, el
because saw I close the end of the journey the

trayecto me pareció corto. A poco de abandonar
way me seemed short At little of to abandon

la estación, vio dibujarse en las sombras de la
the station (I) saw paint itself in the shadows of the

noche la silueta de la enorme mole que
night the silhouette of the enormous mass that

constituía la famosa hacienda de San Javier. Y
constitutes the famous estate of San Javier And

esta silueta, borrosa al principio, fue
that silhouette blurry at the beginning was

definiéndose rápidamente, permitiendo darme
defining itself rapidly permitting to give me

cuenta, primeramente, de la alta chimenea del
count firstly of the high chimney of the

ingenio, después, de la gallarda torre y esbelta
ingenious after of the gallant tower and slender

cúpula de su iglesia, de las troneras de las azoteas
cupola of its church of the pockets of the rooftops

y, en fin, de todos los principales detalles del
and on end of all the principal details of the
finally

edificio.
building

Poco o nada habíamos hablado, y suponiendo
Little or nothing (we) had talked and assuming

que Antonio me enseñaría al día siguiente todos
that Antonio me would teach at the day following all

los pormenores de la hacienda, me abstuve
the details of the estate -myself- (I) abstained

de hacer preguntas; pero, al entrar en el
of to make questions but at the to enter on the
when entering

enorme patio, o más bien plaza, que había delante
enormous patio or more well square that (it) had in front
better called

del edificio, me sorprendió de tal manera la
of the building myself (I) surprised of such manner the
I was surprised

extraña silueta de un hombre sobre el pretil de
strange silhouette of a man on the parapet of

la azotea, que no pude menos que exclamar:
the rooftop that not (I) could less than exclaim

- ¿Quién es ese individuo que espera tu llegada
Who is that individual that awaits your arrival

en tan estrambótica postura?
in such bizarre posture

Porque hay que advertir que estaba sentado sobre
Because has to warn that (he) was seated on

el pretil (con riesgo inminente de caerse), y
the parapet with risk imminent of to fall and

cubierto con el más exagerado sombrero de alta
covered with the most exaggerated hat of high

copa.
cup
(top)

Antonio se río y solamente dijo:
Antonio -himself- laughed and only said

- ¡Ah! Mañana te lo presentaré.
Ah Tomorrow you him (I) will present

Nos apeamos de nuestras caballerías en un
We dismounted from our horses in a

amplio portal, y después de las presentaciones
wide gate and after -of- the presentations

del tenedor de libros y otros dependientes de
of the keeper of books and other dependents of
(employees)

la hacienda, en el "purgar", o sea oficina
the estate in the purge or be (it) (the) office

principal, subimos a tomar una ligerísima cena,
main (we) went down to take a very light dinner

para arrojarnos en seguida en los codiciados
for to throw ourselves in followed in the coveted
then

brazos de Morfeo.
arms of Morpheus
(sleep)

Una pequeña contrariedad se dibujó en el rostro
A small annoyance itself drew on the face

de mi amigo, al informarle el administrador que
of my friend at the inform him the administrator that
when him informed

la mayor parte de las estancias de la casa
the biggest part of the rooms of the house

estaban en vías de reparaciones y de ser
were in ways of reparations and of to be
underway (maintenance)

pintadas, por lo tanto, sólo había disponibles
painted for that much only (it) had available
(there was)

para dormir en ellas, dos habitaciones, una
for to sleep in them two rooms one

pequeña, y otra, al contrario, amplísima. Inútil
small and other at the contrary huge Useless

me parece decir que ésta me fue cedida por mi
me (it) seems to say that that one me was ceded by my

amigo, y al penetrar en ella, grata fue mi
friend and at the to penetrate in her pleasant was my
at entering it

sorpresa al encontrarla muy fresca, y ver
surprise at the to encounter her very cool and to see
at finding it

que la cama se hallaba colocada al lado de
that the bed itself found located at the side of

una puertaventana que comunicaba con el
a door-window that communicated with the

corredor o galería abierta, que abarcaba todo el
corridor or gallery open that spanned all the

frente y un costado del piso superior de la
front and a side of the floor superior of the
(upper)

casa. Medía este corredor unos cuatro metros de
house Half this corridor some four meters of

anchura por otros tantos de elevación, estaba
width for other so many of elevation was
(height)

abovedado, y por los amplios arcos se
vaulted and through the wide arches itself

esbozaba el encantador paisaje, que en las
sketched out the enchanting landscape that in the

sombras de la noche, poseía una dulzura y
shadows of the night possessed a sweetness and

serenidad poco comunes, perfumado el ambiente
serenity little normal perfumed the environment

con las diversas plantas de aquellos climas.
with the various plants of that climates
(region)

A pesar del cansancio que sentía, permanecí no
At weight of the tiredness that (I) felt (I) remained in the

corto espacio de tiempo en la soledad de aquella
short space of time in the solitude of that

galería, perdido en mis pensamientos, y con un
gallery lost in my thoughts and with a

leve zumbar de oídos, "oía el silencio", que sólo
light humming of hearing (I) heard the silence that only

interrumpía, de vez en cuando, el ladrar de
(was) interrupted of time in when (by) the barking of

un perro en el "real" no lejano.
a dog in the reality not far (away)

Por fin me metí entre sábanas, dejando la
For end myself put between sheets leaving the
Finally

ventana abierta, y en seguida quedé dormido.
window open and in followed remained asleep
after that (fell)

No supe cuánto tiempo lo estuviera, cuando me
Not (I) knew how much time it was when me
(what)

despertó el fuerte toser de una persona. Esta
awoke the strong cough of a person That (one)

parecía hallarse en el corredor, a pocos pasos
seemed to find itself in the corridor at few steps

de mí, y deduje en seguida que era el
from me and (I) deduced in followed that (it) was the
then

"velador", que en toda hacienda suele rondar de
watcher that in all estate(s) uses to patrol of
(guard) (at)

noche. Como la tos no cedía, sino, al
night As the cough not stopped but on the

contrario, agravábase de tal manera, que el
contrary worsened itself of such manner that the

pobre hombre parecía correr riesgo de
poor man seemed to run (the) risk of

ahogarse, salté del lecho para prestarle
to choke himself (I) jumped from the bed for to lend him

ayuda; pero ¿cuál no sería mi sorpresa, cuando
help but what not were my surprise when

salí a la galería, de hallar que no sólo cesó
(I) exited at the gallery of to find that not only stopped

la tos, sino que el velador o lo que fuera, no
the cough but that the watcher (guard) or that what (it) was not

se encontraba allí! Torné a acostarme, y a
itself encountered there (I) turned to lay myself down and at

los pocos momentos, se repitió el suceso con
the few moments itself repeated the occurrence with

idénticos resultados, y dos y tres veces más,
identical results and two and three times more

hasta que llegué a suponer que el hombre se
until that (I) arrived to suppose that the man itself

hallaría en algún apartado rincón del corredor,
should find in some separated corner of the corridor

el cual, por ser abovedado, transmitiría el eco
the which for to be vaulted (it) would transmit the echo

de la tos, haciéndola oírse como si fuese en
of the cough making it be heard as if (it) was in

la puerta misma de mi alcoba.
the door same of my bedroom

A la mañana siguiente, relatado el desagradable
At the morning following (when I) told the disagreeable

incidente que interrumpió mi sueño, quiso Antonio
incident that interrupted my sleep wanted Antonio

averiguar quién fuera el velador que había pasado
verify who was the watcher (guard) that had passed

tan mala noche en la galería; pero el
such (a) bad night in the gallery but the

Administrador contestó rotundamente que
administrator answered roundly (assured) that

nadie, pues en aquella época de completa
(it was) no one since in that time of complete

tranquilidad era innecesaria la presencia de
tranquility (it) was unnecessary the presence of

semejante sirviente. Y a las reiteradas instancias
similar servant And at the re-iterated instances (questions)

de que alguien tenía que haber sido, la
of that somebody had that to have been the

contestación, después de ser interrogados todos
answer after of to be interrogated all

los dependientes y criados, fue siempre la
the dependents (inhabitants) and servants was always the

misma.
same

Sin darle más importancia al asunto, pues
Without to give it more importance to the case since

en realidad poco tenía, emprendimos la visita del
in reality little (it) had (we) undertook the visit of the

vasto edificio, remedo de fortaleza, convento y
vast building imitation of fortress convent and

casa de campo, todo en uno, que databa del
house of (the) land all in one that dated from the
manor

siglo XVI; la magnífica iglesia, cuya torre y
century 16th the magnificent church whose tower and

cúpula reverberaban en sus azulejos los rayos del
cupola reverberated in their tiles the rays of the

sol tropical; y la casa de calderas, o ingenio
sun tropical and the house of boilers the ingeniously
boiler house

propiamente dicho, enorme edificio completamente
properly said enormous building completely

moderno y, para mí, ayuno de interés.
modern and for me fasting of interest
(lacking)

Al recorrer la azotea de la casa, Antonio
At the to walk around the rooftop of the house Antonio
When we walked around

hizo la presentación del curioso personaje que
made the presentation of the curious person that
introduced the

la víspera llamara mi atención. ¡Era una
the evening before called my attention (It) was a

estatua de piedra! Y no pude menos que
statue of stone And not (I) could less than

echarme a reír al verla: esculpida con la
to throw myself to laugh at the to see it sculpted with the
(starting) at seeing it

mayor rudeza, representaba a un individuo de
most roughness (it) represented -to- an individual of

anguloso y desproporcionado aspecto, sentado
square and disproportionate aspect seated

al borde de la azotea, con las piernas cruzadas,
at the edge of the rooftop with the legs crossed

más abajo de las rodillas, y con las manos en
more down of the knees and with the hands in

actitud de batir palmas. Para que nada faltase
act of to clap palms For that nothing lacked itself

a esta obra de arte, hallábase embadurnada, desde
to this work of art found itself daubed from

la punta del exagerado sombrero hasta los pies,
the point of the exaggerated hat to the feet

de un brillante color de rosa.
of a brilliant color of pink
(with)

- Aquí tienes, - dijo Antonio, - a la persona
Here (you) have said Antonio -to- the person

que prometí presentarte. Como ves, es una
that (I) promised to introduce to you As (you) see (it) is a

obra de arte. Se llama Herrera Goya. Para que
work of art Itself calls Herrera Goya For that

no te rías de un miembro de la familia,
not yourself (you) laugh of a member of the family

te contaré que Don Joaquín de Herrera Goya
yourself (I) tell that Don Joaquin of Herrera Goya

fue antepasado mío, aunque no en línea recta,
was (an) ancestor (of) mine although not in line direct

pues murió soltero; su hermana, mi cuarta
since (he) died single his sister my quarter

abuela, heredó de él esta hacienda y no
grandmother inherited from him this estate and not

sé si a ella se deba tan hermosa estatua.
(I) know if to her itself owes such (a) beautiful statue

Es costumbre pintarla cada año; así como hoy la
(It) is tradition to paint it each year so as today it

ves color de rosa, ha estado pintada de
(you) see color of pink (it) has been painted of

celeste, amarillo, verde, de todo menos de negro,
sky blue yellow green of all less of black

pues hay aquí la creencia, cosas de los indios,
since has (there is) here the believe thing of the indians

que, si llegara a pintarse de ese color, ocurriría
that if arrives to paint itself of that color would happen

alguna desgracia. La postura de sus manos indica,
some disgrace The posture of his hands indicates

no que va a aplaudir, sino que la distancia
not that (he) goes to appload but that the distance

que con ellos mide es el tamaño de los
that with them (he) measures is the weight (size) of the

panes de azúcar que en su hacienda
breads (bars) of sugar that in his estate

se fabricaban y que llenaron sus bolsillos
themselves fabricate (are produced) and that filled his pockets

de doblones. La tradición no cuenta cosas muy
of (with) doubloons The tradition not tells things very

halagadoras para este señor; te las referiré
flattering for (about) this gentleman yourself them (I) will tell

algún día.
some day

No dejó de caerme en gracia el ridículo
Not (I) let (I stopped) of to fall myself in grace the ridiculous

personaje, y al bajar al patio y verlo
personage and at the go down to the patio and to see him
when going down

desde allí, noté que se hallaba emplazado
from there (I) noted that himself (he) found placed
(he was located)

sobre el corredor, precisamente encima del sitio
on the corridor precisely on top of the site

en donde a aquel daba acceso a la
in where at that (corridor) (it) gave access to the

puertaventana de mi dormitorio.
door-window of my dormitory
(balcony door)

La huerta de la finca, extensa y feraz, llamó mi
The guarden of the estate extensive and fertile called my

atención por su aspecto oriental, debido en gran
attention for its aspect oriental owed in large

parte a una alberca con surtidor que en ella
part to a swimming pool with pump that in her

había. A mi observación contestó Antonio:
(it) had At my observation answered Antonio
(there was)

- Sí. Mi madre la llama "El Jardín de la Sultana".
Yes My mother it calls The garden of the sultana

No te sientes ahí, - agregó al ver que
Not yourself seat here (he) added at the see that
when seeing

me disponía a hacerlo sobre un ancho banco, o
myself (I) disposed to do it on a wide bench or

poyo de piedra, cercano. - Aquí estarás más
stone bench of stone close Here (you) will be more

cómodo.
comfortable

Y al borde mismo del estanque
And at the edge itself of the pool

permanecimos algún tiempo, escuchando el suave
(we) remained some time listening to the gentle

rumor del agua.
sound of the water

No viene al caso referir nuestra vida en aquella
Not (I) come at the case to relate our life in that

finca durante la semana que en ella pasamos; sólo
estate during the week that in her (we) passed only

diré que, durante seis noches, y
(I) will say that during six nights and

aproximadamente a la misma hora, se repitió el
approximately at the same hour itself repeated the

incidente de la primera, cosa que nos intrigó de
incident of the first (night) thing that us intrigued of

tal modo, que nos propusimos descubrir al
such manner that us (we) proposed to discover -to- the

nocturno asmático. Juzgó Antonio lo más acertado
nocturnal asthmatic Judged Antonio the most certain

ordenar a un tal Paulino, muy adicto suyo
to order -to- a such (certain) Paulino very addict (local follower) (of) his

y hombre de toda confianza, que pasara la
and man of total confidence that (he) will pass the

noche en mi estancia, en el umbral mismo de la
night in my room on the threshold itself of the

puertaventana, para ayudar a aclarar el molesto,
door-window for to help to clear up the annoyance

si bien un tanto ridículo misterio.
if well a very ridiculous mystery

Era la última noche que íbamos a pasar en
(It) was the last night that (we) went to spend in

San Javier, puesto que debíamos regresar a México
San Javier since that (we) must return to Mexico

el día siguiente, y me metí en cama con
the day following and myself (I) put in bed with

ánimo de descansar, indiferente al suceso que
(a) mind of to rest indifferent to the success that

tan repetidas veces había turbado mi sueño.
so repeated times had distrubed my sleep

La tos, esa noche, me pareció más fuerte y
The cough that night (to) me seemed more strong and

rebelde que en las anteriores. Al saltar del
rebellious than in the previous (nights) At the jump from the
When jumping

lecho, vi con satisfacción que Paulino también
bed (I) saw with satisfaction that Paulino also

la oía, pues estaba sentado sobre su estera, con
it heard since (he) was seated on his mat with

asombro dibujado en sus facciones. Salimos los
surprise painted on his features (face) (We) exited the (both)

dos y recorrimos la galería, sin encontrar
two and ran around the gallery without to encounter

persona alguna, y con el extraño caso de que
person any and with the strange case of that

el hombre que tosía parecía seguirnos durante
the man that coughed seemed to follow us during

todo el trayecto.
whole the trajectory

Cansados de buscar, regresamos a la estancia, y
Tired of to search (we) returned to the room and

al traspasar el umbral, la tos que el
at the stepping over the threshold the cough that the

misterioso personaje padecía, aumentó de tal
mysterious person suffered augmented of such

manera que oímos claramente que se
manner that (we) heard clearly that himself

ahogaba; esa horrible tos degeneró en ronquido,
(he) choked that horrible cough degenerated in snore

en "estertor", y repentinamente se oyeron
in (death) rattles and all of a sudden themselves heard

maullar, chillar horriblemente, en todas las
to meow (meowing) to shriek (shrieking) horribly in all the

disonancias imaginables, un crecido número de
dissonances imaginable a growing number of

gatos. Yo hubiera jurado que había un centenar
cats I had sworn that (it) had (there were) a hundred

de esos animales alrededor nuestro. Torné a salir
of those animals around us (I) turned to exit

al corredor con la seguridad de ver sus ojos
to the corridor with the certainty of to see their eyes

fosforescentes entre las sombras de la arcada;
phosphorescent between the shadows of the arcade

pero nada se veía. Arreció el horrible
but nothing itself saw Increased the horrible
was seen

desconcierto; oí algo se desplomaba, y
chaos (I) heard something itself collapsed and

al volver la mirada, vi que Paulino, hincado
at the to turn the look (I) saw that Paulino sunk

de rodillas en medio de la estancia, con los
of (his) knees in (the) middle of the room with the
(to)

brazos en cruz, y el mayor terror dibujado en
arms in cross and the largest terror painted on
crossed

su rostro, exclamaba con pavor:
his face exclaimed with fear

- ¡Virgen Santísima! ¡El amo viejo, el amo viejo!
Maiden Holy The master old the master old
The old master

Hay sucesos en la vida, que cuando
Has occurrences in -the- life that when
(There are)

se recuerdan pasados los años y con
themselves remember passed the years and with
they are remembered (after)

espíritu sereno sólo presentan un aspecto risible.
spirit serene only present an aspect laughable

Pero yo jamás olvidaré que aquella noche,
But I never will forget that that night

al oír el estertor de un hombre invisible,
at the to hear the (death) rattle of a man invisible
at hearing

el horrible maullar de cien felinos y los
the horrible meow of (a) hundred felines and the

acentos de terror de un pobre indio, la sangre
accents of terror of a poor indian the blood
(expressions)

se heló dentro de mis venas,
itself froze inside of my veins

erizáronse mis cabellos, se estremeció todo mi
rose themselves my hairs itself shook all my
my hair stood upright

cuerpo, y, lo confieso, ¡tuve miedo!
body and it (I) confess (I) had fear
I was afraid

Salí de la estancia precipitadamente, seguido
(I) exited from the room rushing followed

de Paulino, y tropezando con andamios y botes
by Paulino and tripping with (over) scaffolds and pots

de pintura, fuimos a dar hasta la alcoba en
of paint (we) flew to give (get) to the bedroom in

donde Antonio dormía tranquilo.
where Antonio slept tranquil (with tranquility)

- ¡Antonio, por Dios! - exclamé. - ¡Este lugar está
Antonio by God (I) exclaimed This place is

embrujado!
bewitched (haunted)

- ¿Qué pasa? ¿Qué sucede? ¡Pero, hombre!, -
What passed What happened But man

añadió Antonio, al encender la bujía y ver
added Antonio at the lighting the spark plug and to see

la expresión de nuestros rostros. - ¿Qué
the expression of our faces What

tenéis? ¿Estáis locos?
(do you) have Are (you) mad

- Poco menos, te aseguro.
Little less you (I) assure

Y le referí atropelladamente lo que
And him (I) related hastily it that

acabábamos de oír.
(we) finished of to hear

- ¡Vamos, hombre! ¡No puede ser! Estáis soñando.
Go man Not (it) can be (You) are sleeping

Vamos allá, y verás como no hay nada.
(Let's) go there and (you) will see how not has nothing
(there is)

- ¡No! ¡No vayamos!
Not Not (we) go

- Sí, - dijo resueltamente, y emprendimos la
Yes (he) said resolved and (we) undertook the
(decidedly)

marcha, él por delante. Al llegar a mi
walk he -for- ahead At the to arrive at my
At arriving

dormitorio y penetrar en él, reinaba el mayor
dormitory and to penetrate (entering) in it reigned the greatest

silencio.
silence

- ¿Lo ves? - dijo mi amigo. Pero en ese
It (you) see said my friend But in that

instante se desató de nuevo el maullar
instant itself untied (broke loose) of new the meowing

horrible y Paulino sólo pudo exclamar, con
horrible and Paulino only could exclaim with

acento de terror:
accent (expression) of terror

- Niño, ¡es el amo viejo!
Child (it) is the master old

- ¡Vamos, vámonos de aquí!
(Let's) go (let's) go from here

Y abandonamos aquel pavoroso recinto.
And (we) abandoned that scary enclosure

El resto de la noche lo pasamos Antonio y yo
The rest of the night it (we) passed Antonio and I

sin proferir palabra, en sendas butacas de su
without to utter (a) word in two seats of his

alcoba, fumando cigarrillos y embargadas nuestras
bedroom smoking cigarettes and seized our

mentes con mil conjeturas, hasta que por
minds with (a) thousand conjectures until that through

la abierta ventana vimos desvanecerse las
the open window (we) saw disappear the

estrellas y dibujarse en el cielo la claridad de
stars and paint itself in the sky the clarity of

la ansiada aurora.
the longed for dawn

Como debe suponerse, con la luz del día
As (one) must suppose itself with the light of the day

aumentaron mis deseos de aclarar el extraño
augmented my desires of to clear up the strange

suceso, y asedié a mi amigo con mil
occurrence and (I) besieged -to- my friend with (a) thousand

preguntas, a las que él se excusaba de
questions at those (which) that he himself excused of

contestar, diciendo que todo era también un
to answer saying that all was also a

misterio para él. Pero a pesar de ello, me
mystery for him But at weight (in spite) of that myself

convencí de que algo sabía que no quería
(I) convinced of that something knew that not (he) wanted

comunicarme, y tanto le insté, que,
to communicate to me and so much to him (I) insisted that

al fin, requirió del Administrador unas
at the end (he) required from the administrator some

vetustas llaves, y dijo lacónicamente:
ancient keys and (he) said laconically

- Sígueme.
Follow me

Atravesamos todo el corredor, risueño con la luz
(We) traversed all the corridor smiling with the light

matinal y el perfume de las plantas que allí
of the morning and the perfume of the plants that there

había; bajamos escaleras, recorrimos pasillos,
(it) had (we) went down stairs walked through passages
(were there)

y, por fin, Antonio abrió una pequeña puerta,
and for end Antonio opened a small door
(at the)

que, al girar en sus goznes, dejó escapar un
that at the turn in its hinges let escape a
(turning)

fuerte olor a papel y badana viejos. En seguida
strong smell of paper and sheepskin old In followed
old sheepskin Then

comprendí que era el archivo de la casa. En
understood (I) that (it) was the archive of the house In

efecto, hallábase aquella abovedada cámara
effect (it) found itself that vaulted chamber
(it was located)

repleta de legajos, infolios y libros, hacinados en
filled of files books and books crammed on
(with) {folios}

varios estantes y cuidadosamente ordenados,
various shelves and carefully ordered

según podía colegirse por los claros
according to (it) could conclude oneself by the clear

números y letreros que cada uno ostentaba.
numbers and letters that each one displayed

Detúvose un instante, y recorrió con la
(He) halted himself an instant and roamed with the

vista aquel vetusto arsenal de papel y pergamino.
sight that ancient arsenal of paper and parchment

Extendió el brazo, y bajó de su sitio un
(He) extended the arm and lowered from its site a

legajo de no grandes dimensiones; lo desató
file of not great dimensions it (he) untied

cuidadosamente y repasó los expedientes que
carefully and reviewed the records that

contenía, hasta dar con un edicto del
(it) contained until to give (to encounter) with an edict of the

Santo Oficio, escrito en recio papel de Génova y
Saintly Office written in strong paper of Genoa and

encabezado con la consabida fórmula de "Nos los
headed with the well-known formula of Us the

Inquisidores de la Fe contra la herética
inquisitors of the Faith against the heretic

bravedad etc.". Algún tiempo tardé en descifrar
boldness etc Some time (he) delayed in to decipher

su contenido, sacando en conclusión, que el 15
its contents drawing in conclusion that the 15th

de Agosto del año de 1614, fue denunciado como
of August of the year of 1614 was denounced as

brujo, ante el Santo Oficio de la Inquisición, el
witch before the Saintly Office of the Inquisition the

Señor don Joaquín de Herrera Goya, dueño de la
Lord don Joaquin of Herrera Goya master of the

"Hacienda de Moler azúcar de San Francisco
Estate of Moler sugar of (by) San Francisco

Xavier, Obispado de la Puebla de los Angeles". El
Xavier Bishop of the Village of the Angels The

temido tribunal citaba a dicho señor a
feared tribunal cited to said gentleman to

comparecer ante él, por tan horrible cargo, y,
appear before him for such horrible charge and

en caso de hallarse culpable, sufrir la pena
in case of to find himself guilty to suffer the penalty

consiguiente.
subsequent

- ¡Mal lo pasaría Herrera Goya en el Santo
Bad that passed Herrera Goya in the Saintly

Oficio! - exclamé, al terminar la lectura
Office (I) exclaimed at the end (ending) (of) the lecture (reading)

del documento.
of the document

- No compareció, - dijo Antonio. - El día en que
Not (he) appeared said Antonio The day in that

recibió este edicto, murió.
(he) received this edict (he) died

- ¡Cómo! ¿De qué manera?
How Of what manner
In what way

- Yo creo que murió de viejo, tenía ochenta
I believe that (he) died of old (age) (he) had eighty

años, o del susto de hallarse en tan apurado
years or of the shock of to find himself in such troubled

trance; aunque te diré, puesto que todo
state although you (I) will say put that all

quieres saberlo, que hay quien dice que su
(you) want to know that has (those) who say that his
(there are)

muerte fue trágica. Este Herrera Goya, según
death was tragic This Herrera Goya according to

parece, era un ente raro, sobre todo para su
(what it) seems was a fellow strange over all for his

época. Solía hacer experimentos con yerbas,
time (He) used to do experiments with herbs

coleccionaba insectos, y tenía hasta medio
collected insects and had up to half

centenar de gatos, que lo seguían por todos
(a) hundred of cats that him followed at all

lados.
sides

No dejó de causarme desagradable sorpresa este
Not (it) let of to cause me disagreeable surprise this
(it lacked)

extremo, que relacionó en seguida con el
extreme (thing) that (he) told in followed with the
next

misterio que deseábamos aclarar.
mystery that (we) desired to clear up

- Comprendo tu sobresalto, - continuó Antonio. -
(I) understand your surprise continued Antonio

Y has de saber que, según la tradición
And (you) have -of- to know that according to the tradition

entre la gente de esta hacienda, Herrera Goya,
between the people of this estate Herrera Goya

el Amo Viejo, como le llaman, maltrataba
the master old as him (they) called maltreated
old master

sobremanera a su extraño séquito; es más, lo
especially -to- his strange following (it) is more it
(them)

martirizaba a cada momento. Y aseguran
(he) tortured at each moment And (they) ascertained

que, cuando murió, fue porque todos sus gatos
that when (he) died (it) was because all his cats

se le echaron encima, clavándole las uñas
themselves him threw on top scratching him the nails

en el cuello, y desgarrándole la garganta en
in the neck and tearing of him the throat in

girones, hasta dejarlo, después de horribles
shreds until to leave him after of horrible

sufrimientos, exánime en un charco de su propia
sufferings lifeless in a puddle of his own

sangre.
blood

Refirióme luego cómo el Santo Oficio de la
(I) referred myself later how the Saintly Office of the

Inquisición prohibió que se enterrase a
Inquisition prohibited that himself was buried -to-

Herrera en lugar sagrado y cómo fue inhumado
Herrera in (a) place sacred and how was buried

el sangriento cadáver en la huerta, en donde
the bloody corpse in the garden in where

marcaba su sepultura lo que yo había confundido
marked his grave that what I had confused

con un asiento.
with a seat

En la tarde de ese día emprendimos el regreso
On the afternoon of that day (we) undertook the return

a México, y durante todo el trayecto, no pude
to Mexico and during whole the trajectory (trip) not (I) could

distraer de mi mente el suceso que tanto me
distract from my mind the happening that so much me

había impresionado. Al llegar a la ciudad,
had impressed At the arrive at the city
At arriving

mandé decir misas por el alma de aquel "amo
(I) ordered to say masses for the soul of that master

viejo", a quien se le negó cristiana
old to whom itself to him (was) refused (a) Christian

sepultura, aunque la halló poética, cobijada por
burial although it (I) found poetic covered by

manglares y palmeras, cerca del surtidor del
mangroves and palm trees close of the pump of the

"Jardín de la Sultana".
Garden of the Sultana

Pasaron algunos meses. Un día me dijo Antonio:
(There) passed some months One day me said Antonio

- ¿Sabes que he escrito a San Javier,
(You) know that (I) have written to San Javier

ordenando que este año se pinte a Herrera
ordening that this year itself paints -to- Herrera

Goya de negro?
Goya -of- black

- ¡Hombre, no hagas eso! Ten prudencia.
Man not do that Have care

- ¡Hola! ¿Eres supersticioso?
Hello Are (you) superstitious

Tres días después, la sociedad de México quedó
Three days after the society of Mexico remained

consternada, al saber que las hordas rebeldes
in consternation at the know that the hordes (of) rebels

habían entrado a saco en la hacienda principal de
had entered to sack in the estate main of

los Hernández Sandoval, que habían prendido
the Hernandez Sandoval that (they) had taken

fuego a su ingenio, y volado con dinamita el
fire to his ingenuity and flown with dynamite the
(brilliant work) (blown up)

vetusto edificio.
ancient building

San Javier ya no era más que un enormе
San Javier already not was more than a enormous

montón de escombros.
mountain of rubbish

www.ingramcontent.com/pod-product-compliance
Lightning Source LLC
LaVergne TN
LVHW011324080426
835513LV00006B/181